Stop selling books nobody buys

STOP SELLING BOOKS NOBODY BUYS

Four effective strategies to use your business book to attract ideal clients on autopilot (without shouting "buy my book")

DEBBIE JENKINS

Book Interior and E-book Design by
Amit Dey | amitdey2528@gmail.com

To find out more about our authors and books visit:
www.intellectualperspective.com

This book is enhanced with additional video content, checklists, playbooks, case studies and discussions. You can access all of this extra content by signing up at: www.ShortValuableBooks.com

This is book two in the "Ideas Into Assets" series. Book one is *Stop writing books nobody reads*. You'll also get advance reading of the next books in the series when you sign up, plus more information, techniques, tactics and ideas about how to turn your thoughts into valuable things, along with free access to a community of creators and leaders.

I debated putting the word "that" into the title (*Stop selling books* that *nobody buys*) but in the pursuit of brevity, and with the assumption that you're reading this to learn, not check my grammar, I decided you didn't need that that.

CONTENTS

PRAISE FOR STOP SELLING BOOKS NOBODY BUYS

I wish I'd read this before my books were published. It is wonderful to write and publish a book but it is even better if people buy it. If you read this brilliant book it will show you how to write what people want to buy.

Geoff Burch, The Legendary Alternative Business Guru
(and the reason I started in business)

She's done it again. Debs Jenkins is really turning into the 'go-to girl' for anybody interested in getting their ideas out to a wider audience.

Piers Fallowfield-Cooper,
Author of *Are You Still The Future?*

The thing I love about Debbie Jenkins and each book she writes is that she lives what she writes. She doesn't test it on you, the reader. The engineer in her just wouldn't let her. She figures out how to first write a book that people will want to read (book 1) and then she figures out how to make it do the job you wanted it to (book 2). I love that she'll make you realise that it's not just the sales you're after, which she'll show you how to do in this book. She also wants you to make that transformational impact on the reader that changes their lives and their business. And more, she wants your book to change your life and business too. That's the bit where she truly focused my mind.

She is grounded, creative, and practical and will make you think about marketing your book in a way you never thought of. It's so simple and so clever you'll bring her book with you every-where you go so you don't miss a trick. I imagine it's like having a little Debbie in your pocket who pinches you just when you need pinching, with a little giggle to boot. Buy this book. It'll help other people buy yours!

Finola Howard,
Marketing & Brand Positioning Strategist

Stop Selling Books Nobody Buys is an absolute practical revela-tion! With smart strategies to effortlessly attract clients and a refreshing approach that goes beyond the ordinary, this book is a game-changer for anyone seeking to thrive in conveying and maximizing the value of their book. Debbie's expertise shines through every page, a testament to her brilliance as an author and booksmith!

Olivier Van Duüren, Visual Sensemaker and (co)
author of *Transforming while Performing: How Organisations can find their North Star* and *Get Everyone to Act in Days, not Months*

Utterly brilliant, simple hyper-personalised and authentic strat-egies to get your book in the hands of more business leaders!

Karen Currier,
Author of *DOING intentionally*

Stop Selling Books Nobody Buys is a practical and easy-to-read guide that challenges business authors to consider the job their book has to do, packed with practical, hands-on advice.

It introduces a series of key strategies to sell your book as a solution. As such it serves as a compass for both seasoned authors and those aspiring to enter the world of writing, offering insights and options to publish and steer you in the right direction. I found it particularly beneficial as I read it when we were in the midst of launching our own book.

Kristof Braekeleire, Visual Sensemaker and (co)
author of *Transforming while Performing:
How Organisations can find their North Star* and
Get Everyone to Act in Days, not Months

This is a great little no-nonsense book, packed with tips and humour. Not only did I read it cover to cover (making me very late for an event!) I also have pages full of notes I now need to organise. Curse you, Debs!
I shall be following this playbook with my next book. If you see it, it is a testament to these techniques.
Strong recommendation for any current or aspiring authors.

Callum Laing, Founder & Chair MBH
Corporation PLC and multiple author

Seems like everybody is writing books these days: often by rehashing other people's stuff, or even getting 'AI' to rehash other people's stuff. That means that if you've genuinely got valuable ideas to communicate in print, you need to be good at more than writing. Debbie Jenkins knows what you need, and in 'Stop Selling Books Nobody Buys' she lays it out. There are publishing and book marketing truths, pitfalls and solutions here that most of her audience won't even have guessed about. If you need your book to succeed, then you need this book.

Andy Bass, Author of *Start With What Works*
and *Committed Action*

Thinking of writing a book? Don't! Not until you read Debs Jenkins' new book, Stop Selling Books Nobody Buys! A book is a lot of work and of little value if you aren't clear about why you are writing it, what you are going to do with it, and how you are going to get it into the hands of those who need to read it.

Ann Latham, Author of *The Power of Clarity* and
The Disconnect Principle

Debs has been my marketing guru since I set up my business in 2005. Stop Selling Books Nobody Buys is packed full of pragmatic, easy-to-implement solutions, which is written in her usual humorous but deadly serious, researched-backed style.

Estelle Read, Author of *Inner Brilliance · Outer Shine: 10 Antidotes to Imposter Syndrome, Workaholism & Stress* and Speaker at Beee

If, like me, you are a good writer, a quick thinker and a slow learner when it comes to getting your books to those who need them, you might be relieved to discover Stop Selling Books Nobody Buys. It is chock full of helpful insights and is designed (unsurprisingly, very well designed given Debs Jenkin's earlier engineering career) so you can construct a straightforward system that works for you - so that people get to read your book! Not only do we authors need to write interesting well-designed books that respect readers' needs for accessible information, practical techniques and strategies that might not have crossed their minds, but we also need to employ the same level of thoughtfulness and design in the process of getting the word out to our potential audiences.

Judy Barber,
Author of *The Slow Coach Approach*

Another insightful, inspiring and informative read from Debbie. I have come to expect value on every page of Debbie's books and this one doesn't disappoint. Having just written my first book in one of her cohort publishing masterminds, these strategies are exactly what I need to get my book into the hands of my ideal clients. No matter how you feel about marketing and selling you will discover a strategy that works for you and will make all that hard work worthwhile.

Susannah Simmons, Software Adoption Doctor and Author of *The Mystery of the Lost Customer*

Debbie clearly tells you exactly what to do: Write a book that solves the reader's problem. In business startup language, you need to offer an aspirin to relieve the reader's pain. Jenkins tells you how to do this. After reading this book, you will understand why books with impressive titles sit on store shelves. If you follow Debbie's advice, your book will get bought and read. And you will be entertained by phrases like "faster than a caffeinated cat on a mission." Buy her book, follow her process and people will buy your book.

Dan Kowalski, Author of *W.I.S.E Choices at Work*

1. YOU'VE WRITTEN A BOOK, NOW WHAT? YOU KNEW THAT WASN'T THE END OF YOUR WORK, RIGHT?

What do we want?

A book that is read and referred,[1] searched for and shared, desired and devoured.

When do we want it?

Now!

What are we prepared to do to get it?

Usually very little.

What do we want?	A book that is read and referred, searched for and shared, desired and devoured.
When do we want it?	Now!
What are we prepared to do to get it?	Usually very little.

Joking aside, I know you're prepared to do what it takes because you've already done the incredible. You've achieved the seemingly impossible feat of crossing the brain ⚡ world barrier. You've wrestled ideas from your mind and fashioned them into a visible creation. Your book, your brainchild, now lives outside of your head for all to see. Here comes the challenging question: how am I going to get my book into the hands of the people who need it?

This moment often causes one of two pitfalls:

1. The publish and hope mentality – "If I write it, they will come."
2. The fear of becoming a broken record – "I can't possibly talk about my book anymore!"

The second pitfall usually emerges from the lack of a marketing plan and a sprinkle of inexperience, while the first pitfall stems from a belief that everybody is watching you, and that you are, in fact, the star of the show. (You're wrong, it's me, I'm the star![2]) Either pitfall can stop your book from fulfilling its mission – to demonstrate your authority and reach the right audience.

Marketing is a way of informing the right people about something that will benefit them. Yes, the creation process is magical, but it's through distribution and sharing that you truly make a difference and everyone wins.

I want to convince you that selling your book one at a time is only one strategy for making an impact. There are three other strategies that you might not have thought about that could get you there faster and easier.

The goal for this book? To help you navigate this marketing journey successfully, avoid those treacherous pitfalls to steer clear of a marketing catastrophe, and set a clear, effective marketing direction instead.

If you take only one idea away from this book I want it to be: stop selling the book, sell the idea in the book that solves the problem the reader has. You'll make your life infinitely simpler.

As an ex-engineer I'm pretty good at building things, you should see me wielding my soldering iron. With my pen or keyboard, it's no different. I use my engineering background and love for writing to design non-fiction books and marketing plans. When you're assembling a circuit board each component, from the smallest resistor to the largest capacitor, has its specific function and place. You can't randomly solder them together; there needs to be a plan, a schematic. That's what I'm sharing here. This book isn't only filled with facts and figures, principles and protocols, outlines and order, rules and recommendations but also stories, metaphors and creativity. This should make learning more enjoyable and less of a chore.

Getting your book in front of the right people is a systematic process *and* an art.

Here's the first metaphor to wrap your head around. Imagine your business book is a pot of soup cooking on the stove. Your goal is to bring this soup (your book) to a delicious, bubbling simmer (your sales goal).

The heat from the stove represents your marketing efforts. When you turn up the heat (increase your marketing efforts), the soup begins to warm up (interest in your book grows). The higher the heat, the quicker it gets to that perfect simmer.

Now, here's where hysteresis comes in (I warned you about the engineer bit). You already know what hysteresis means but might not realise it. It goes like this, just like in a real pot of soup, the heat doesn't instantly translate to temperature. If you've been keeping the heat low, and suddenly crank it up, it will take a while for the soup to respond. Similarly, if you've been blasting the heat and quickly turn it off, the soup doesn't instantly cool – it keeps simmering for a while.

In the world of selling your business book, this means that increasing your marketing efforts, the "hot" moments (attracting incoming leads) won't lead to an immediate spike in sales (payoff). Conversely, if you pull back on marketing, the "cold" moments,, sales won't instantly plummet. There's always a bit of a delay.

But, just like with soup, the key is to find that perfect temperature and keep it steady. Too little heat, and your soup never simmers. Too much heat, and it could boil over and make a mess. Too little marketing might mean your book never gets noticed, but too much could overwhelm or turn off potential readers.

You can see on the marketing hysteresis graph, that when you are making strategic offers and turning up the heat you increase the incoming interest and the payoff. When you slow down or turn off the heat, you reduce your incoming and the payoff.

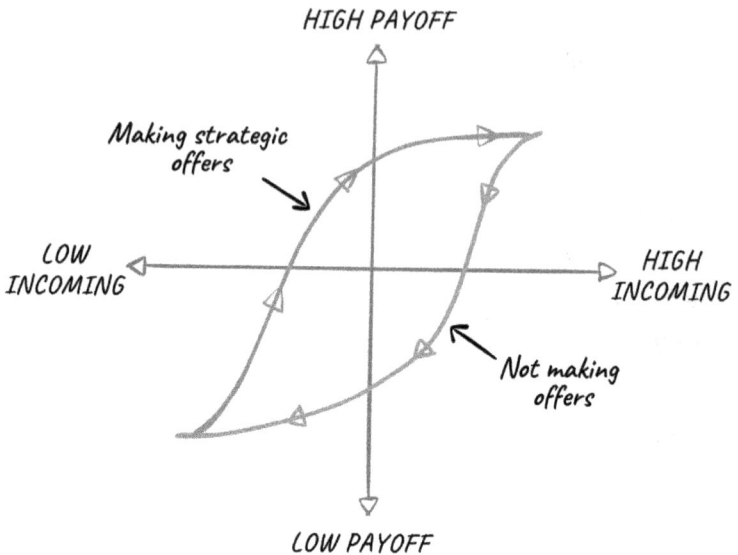

So, your job as the chef (or the marketer) is to keep a close eye on that pot, adjust the heat as necessary, and stir occasionally to make sure everything is evenly heated and nothing sticks to the bottom.

I want you to keep this idea firmly in your head as we discuss the ways you can get your book into the hands of the people who need to read it. That might be by selling. I'm certainly not against selling and the first strategy talks all about it. There are other ways to turn the heat up, and you might not even know about them.

Finally, you need to monitor your marketing strategies, adjust them based on results, and ensure you're reaching all potential readers. With a little patience and careful attention, you'll have a successful business book that's "well cooked".

The usual suspects

I joke that there are at least 1,763 things you could do to market your book. Some of them will work. The problem you have is finding enough time, money and resources to test and experiment. This means you'll probably just model the ones you've seen other people do. I talk more about this problem in strategy three.

> In this book I'm trying to avoid using the words "selling" and "marketing" as much as possible. They conjure up bad memories for most business owners, and fear for others. For simplicity I'm going to say "moving your book". Moving your book into the hands of the people who need to read it so they will get the result you promised and will then refer your book, and want to work with you.

You can make your life easier if you have a book that people want to read[3]. Alex Hormozi[4] on The Danny Miranda Podcast[5]: *"I would rather spend two years building an exceptional product, then let all the customers of that book spend the rest of their lives promoting that for me, than spend two months making a decent book and then have to spend the rest of my life promoting it because no one else wants to do it for me."*

Before you even think about ways of moving your book do a quick sanity check.

If your book:

- ✓ Has a job to do for your business (chapter 2)
- ✓ Solves a problem for one real reader/buyer (chapter 2)
- ✓ Is so valuable people won't stop talking about it

Then all you need to do is:

- Be visible where "they" are ("they" are at different stages in your marketing flow – suspects, prospects, expects, referrers – coming up next and in strategy one)
- Use other people's time, money and network (social, guesting, partnership – strategy two)
- Get to "owned" as quickly as possible (build that list – strategy three)
- Be direct, enthusiastic and targeted (personalised special send outs – strategy four)
- Then reuse, recycle, upcycle (set everything on a fly-wheel so you can write that next book)

Your dream of sharing your valuable insights and experiences through a business book is within your grasp. Even though previous attempts to market your book have not been as successful as you would like, that's not a failure on your part. You simply may not have had the right techniques or strategies at your disposal. It's perfectly natural to have fears about marketing and reaching your target audience, but remember, every successful author has been in your shoes. I feel that fear with every book. You know your book can truly make a difference for other business professionals, and you're right. Your book holds the potential to guide and inspire many. To make your dream a reality, let me help you put an end to the lukewarm marketing that's preventing your book from reaching the people who need to hear your message.

That way you don't have to run around shouting "buy my book!"

Problems with the hot and cold "strategy"

First of all it's not much of a strategy really. It's more wishful thinking coupled with a bit of panic that you've wasted your time and effort. I know that feeling. You're not alone.

Not only that, but there are also distinct marketing phases over the lifetime of a book. You need to have a strategy for all of the phases. You might change strategies for different phases:

1. Pre-launch and during writing: your strategy will be around getting visible on social media, collecting a Book Lovers Team around you to help with marketing, and growing your mailing list.

2. Launch: get sales by making people an offer they can't refuse, promotional pricing, and getting a bestseller.

3. Post-launch and upcycling: keep the boil by getting those reviews in, serialising the ideas from the book, and being visible.

You don't have to only do one launch. You can do a soft launch, a second launch, your birthday launch or a Valentine's Day launch. You can make up as many different reasons for doing a launch as you wish. You will then be able to re-use all your launch assets, like the email sequences and images. So don't worry about putting all of your efforts into this first one. There are no launch police.

Constantly oscillating between "hot" and "cold" in terms of marketing and promotion can lead to several problems for a business book author who aims to grow their business and improve influence. Here are some of the key issues:

1. Lack of consistency: inconsistent marketing efforts can make it difficult for potential readers to remember and recognise your book. Who are you again? This inconsistency can lead to missed opportunities for building a strong brand, which is essential for growing a business and improving influence.

2. Ineffective use of resources: constantly switching between marketing activities can lead to inefficient use of time, money and effort. This can lead to pants[6] results, as resources are not being allocated to the most effective strategies. In fact, you never even find out what the most effective strategies are.

3. Difficulty building momentum: the success of a book launch often depends on the momentum

generated during the promotion period. By constantly moving between hot and cold periods even during the launch, it becomes difficult to build and maintain that momentum, which can hinder the book's overall success. You need to launch your book and keep it at the boil. The simmer is as important as the boil.

4. Loss of reader interest: readers may lose interest in the book if they think you've moved onto another subject. This can lead to a decrease in sales, less word-of-mouth promotion, and ultimately, a weaker impact on your business and influence. This happened to me with my Spain books: I stopped being consistent and the sales went down.

5. Inability to establish credibility: a well-executed marketing campaign can help establish your credibility and expertise. However, constantly switching between marketing strategies can make it challenging to convey a consistent message and establish a strong reputation.

6. Limited long-term success: in order to grow a business and improve influence, it's important to focus on long-term success. An inconsistent marketing approach may lead to short-lived spikes in interest, but it will not provide the sustained growth necessary for achieving long-term goals.

To avoid these problems you need to develop a consistent, well-planned marketing strategy that effectively utilises resources and builds momentum. This will help create a strong brand, engage readers, and ultimately contribute to the growth and success of your business and influence.

The strategies I'm going to share in the book can be used to get to the boil and keep the simmer going over a long time. Some books might even last your lifetime.

Challenges in this sixty second world

In 2022, I wrote *Stop writing books nobody reads*, and jokingly mentioned that in 2022 the average time spent on TikTok was 52 minutes.[7] According to the latest data, US adults spend the most time on TikTok, averaging 55.8 minutes a day on the platform in 2023.[8] The number of minutes spent watching crazy cats is eating into the time you have to get the attention of people. It's only going to get worse.

In 2023, it is estimated that approximately 120 zettabytes of data will be created, transformed, captured, copied, and consumed globally during the year.[9] This amount is expected to more than double from 2022 to 2026, with the enterprise datasphere (all the business data created, captured, replicated and consumed) growing more than twice as fast as the consumer datasphere (all the cat videos you've watched) over the next five years.[10]

So, 120 zettabytes is equal to 120 billion billion (120,000,000,000,000,000,000,000) bytes. If we divide this by 3,000, we get approximately 40 quintillion (40,000,000,000,000,000,000,000) pages[11]. If these pages were laid end-to-end, they could stretch from Earth to the Sun and back approximately 13.5 million times. And if you were an incredibly speedy reader who could finish a 300-page book (don't do it, read short valuable books) in just one hour, it would take you about 152 billion billion (152,000,000,000,000,000,000) years to read 120 zettabytes of data. That's over 11,000 times the current age of the universe, so you'd better get started!

In terms of content creation on social media, Facebook has a significant volume of daily active users, reaching 1.98 billion in the third quarter of 2022, which was a 3% increase year-over-year.[12] Facebook also received 11.2 billion visits, with an average visit time of 31 minutes, indicating a large volume of content creation and consumption on the platform.

In summary, both the amount of data created daily and the content created on social media are experiencing significant growth, with varying rates of growth across different platforms and types of data.

> The amount of data up for consumption is ginormous and growing fast. You are competing with a tsunami of information. Your potential audience has a lot of options. If you want to make your book an easy selection, then make it important to them.

In the last half of 2022 and the start of 2023 a new factor was added that will increase the rate of data creation – generative AI.[13] ChatGPT, Bard, Notion AI, and a petabyte of other little helpers can churn out content faster than a caffeinated cat on a mission.

You are not only competing for attention with books, other forms of media (short form video, podcasts, blogs, etc.) and real life, you're now competing against the robots, and the people using the robots (me).

> Remember, AI is not a replacement for thinking and writing. It is your helpful sidekick, not your overlord. You're still in charge – asking the right questions, making the final calls and reaping the benefits of speedy assistance. My little AI buddy (called Buddy) is an aid for the writing and marketing process. I'm the Boss (I get him to call me Boss, I'm not an egomaniac, really). I still direct the ideas, formulate useful prompts and make the final decisions – Buddy just gets me there faster.

Jeff Hammerbacher, a data scientist and cofounder at Cloudera, says: *"The best minds of my generation are thinking about how to make people click ads."* The data is not just created to get your attention, but to get your consideration and clicks. Most people have something to sell and they want you to buy it. Their outcome is a transfer of your dollars to their pockets.

Those same brilliant minds are now coupled with GenAI interns, and the rate of attention grabbing content is only increasing.

You have the same issue. You have a book you want people to buy. "They" know that, and just like you their guard is raised. If you could get your book into the right hands without selling, how much easier would your job be – and how much more fun?

You don't need to be a YouTubing TikToker to get your book in the hands of the people who need to read it. You need to add value. Of course, if your readers value the YouTube and TikTok channels, **and go on to read afterwards**, then get your camera and lights out and make that short form video. If not, go where they are, add value and be useful – stop making noise.

Endnotes

1. If you haven't written a book, or your book isn't getting read and referred, you might enjoy reading my first book in the Ideas into Assets Series, **Stop writing books nobody reads**. You can get a copy at www.ShortValuableBooks.com

2. In fact, the person you can help by solving their problem is *the* star. It might be me!

3. And, luckily for you there's a book to help you with that: *Stop writing books nobody reads*. You can get a copy from www.shortvaluablebooks.com

4. Hormozi broke a World Record with his book launch for $100M Leads in August, 2023 with an offer that was so good you'd be stupid not taking him up on it.
https://www.youtube.com/watch?v=qel9bf653Es

5. Alex Hormozi: Reprogram Your Mind To Win | The Danny Miranda Podcast 377 - https://www.youtube.com/watch?v=wKQiy_cA6OA&t=4362s

6. The average time spent on TikTok per day in 2022 was fifty-two minutes worldwide: https://backlinko.com/tiktok-users

7. AVERAGE TIME SPENT ON SOCIAL MEDIA IN 2023 (BY PLATFORM) https://www.oberlo.com/statistics/average-time-spent-on-social-media

8. Technical term for bad. I intend to use the word pants in all my books.

9. How Much Data is Generated Every Day in 2023?

    https://increditools.com/how-much-data-is-generated-every-day/

10. Worldwide IDC Global DataSphere Forecast, 2022–2026: Enterprise Organizations Driving Most of the Data Growth – https://www.idc.com/getdoc.jsp?containerId=US49018922

11. 1 byte is roughly equivalent to one character of text, including spaces and punctuation. On average, a page of a book might have around 500 words, and assuming an average word length of 5 characters plus a space, we get about 3,000 characters or bytes per page.

12. 500+ Social Media Statistics You Must Know in 2023 https://www.socialpilot.co/blog/social-media-statistics

13. If you haven't heard of GenAI you might be the only person in the world, along with my mom. GenAI is like a very smart computer program that can create new things, like stories or pictures, all by itself.

2. IT'S NOT ONLY ABOUT THE SALE – YOUR BOOK HAS A JOB TO DO

The book *sale* isn't the important part. This might be a surprising notion, especially in a world where success is so often equated with numbers. But when it comes to non-fiction business books, the transaction is only a small part of the story. A sale does not necessarily equate to influence or impact. After all, what is the point of a sale if the book goes unread, if its wisdom remains unheeded, its strategies unimplemented?

Your book has a job to do. And it's not just to be purchased, but to be used. The value of a business book lies not in the volume of sales, but in the transformation for the reader. When your reader applies the principles laid out in your book and when those applications result in tangible improvements, that's when you know your book has done its job. Your book is not just a product – it's a tool, a resource, a catalyst for change.

I'm not against selling books – I bloody love it. There's an undeniable thrill in knowing that your thoughts, your insights, your hard work, are resonating with people enough for them to want to own a piece of it. But I am against outdated sales and marketing tactics that rely on measuring the number of sales of a book to gauge its success. Such metrics are reductive, failing to capture the full picture of a book's value and influence. **The worth of your book should not be dictated by a sales count, but by the impact it has on the reader, and in turn, on their business or on them.**

> **People don't buy books. They buy solutions to problems.**

Why did you write the book in the first place?

You wrote your book for a purpose. It has a job to do for them and for you.[1]

One of those jobs, perhaps the most important, is to advance and enhance the stages of the relationship you have with the people who need your solution. Your book can take potential clients from attention to consideration to monetary exchange. There are four stages of enhancing a relationship with a client or customer:

1. Suspects: The people you suspect may want what you have. You generate leads for your business by getting their Attention (A on the image).

2. Prospects: The self-proclaimed prospects (they put their hand up) are interested and get to know, like

and trust you. You nurture your relationship with them by getting their Information, in return for giving them Information.

3. Expects: You deliver valuable services and products to people who come to expect a level of attention, and you reward their loyalty with more brilliant assets. You get paid for this – Money. These are your clients.

4. Referrers: Make it easy, pleasant and profitable (not only in cash) to refer you, so they spread awareness and you don't have to shout about yourself. You've captured their hearts.

Stages of Communication

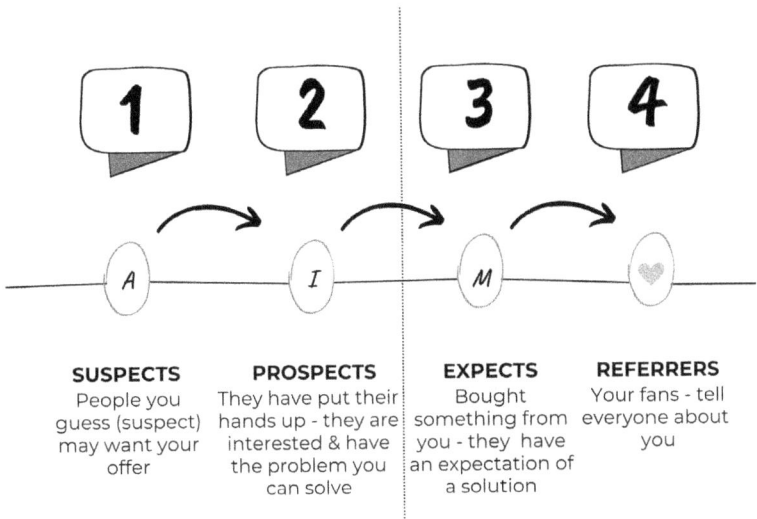

SUSPECTS	PROSPECTS	EXPECTS	REFERRERS
People you guess (suspect) may want your offer	They have put their hands up - they are interested & have the problem you can solve	Bought something from you - they have an expectation of a solution	Your fans - tell everyone about you

On the left you are paying for the relationship; on the right they are paying for the value you have provided. On the left you have negative return on investment (ROI) and it only turns positive when you move people over that line. Your goal is to get people to the right-hand side quickly and efficiently. You do that with an offer.

> **Your marketing can turn people off too. They might not like you. That's OK, they're not your people. Vanilla might be loved universally, yet it's not everyone's favourite flavour. Embrace your unique essence, attract those who crave your distinct taste, and let your marketing reflect your authentic you.**

This is marketing 101. I call it **AIM** ♥ marketing (Attention, Information, Money, Hearts), and without it you have aimless marketing. (This is my one and only apology for puns throughout the book!)

How does your book advance the STAGE of communication?

What job does your book do? Does it get attention and stop the scroll on the socials? Will you give it away in return for their email address to build your list of prospects? Will it be your first product to turn prospects into "expects" and receive money for value? Perhaps it will help current clients become evangelists and referrers? You decide. Your book can do any of those jobs (which is why books are so great).

In addition, your book should have an outcome for your business. If you don't have an outcome for your book, how will you know if it was successful? How will you know if you need to course correct? I always consider these three outcomes when I am deciding what job my book has to do:

1. Save you time/money: Your book could be a useful onboarding tool so clients know what to expect when they work with you. You could use it to reduce ambiguity, so everyone understands your procedures or frameworks. Your book could be the best "credibility clue" reducing the time and effort needed to turn prospects into happy expects (clients).

2. Generate revenue: Your book could be a new product to sell or generate qualified leads to sell to. It could be part of an upsell or downsell for your other business assets and products, and add extra value to existing customers. Or it could create credibility clues to increase referrals.

3. Increase the value of your business: If you are looking to sell or find funding for your business, or you're looking for a partner then the value of your business is important. Your book can attract qualified leads, generate ongoing revenue and royalties, and can be an asset for many years – if you do it right.

What outcome does your book create for you?

The job to be done: Your book can help communicate with the people you want to influence and do business with and it can save time or money, generate revenue or increase the value of your business. For the rest of the book I'm going to assume you know the job your book is doing for you. I suggest you write it down and remind yourself of your decision before every marketing activity.

What options do you have available? More than you think.

The options you have for marketing and selling your book depend on the publishing route you chose and the assets you have available.

Traditional publishing houses set the sales numbers game up – their only goal is to sell books. They are looking for bestsellers, and they want you (the author) to have a huge platform and the ability to sell thousands of books. **Their focus is on you becoming a salesperson for your book – a salesperson for the publisher.** You get your 15% sales commission.[1]

The traditional publishers have their own goals. They are not *always* aligned with yours. If you wanted a sales job you'd have started a company. (Oops, you probably have, but at least you make sales for you!)

The service-based publishing models – such as paid for publishing and self-publishing professionals (because you don't do "self-publishing" on your own) are paid a fee and you own all rights and all royalties. **Your business models are aligned on a transaction and you get the most control of your assets**, giving you the widest options for sales and marketing.

The disadvantage is that they have no vested interest in whether your book is good, useful and beneficial to the reader or to you. They just want the transaction. Then the next.

With the majority of hybrid publishers (and the reason for the name) **you get to pay for a service and share the equity**, frequently a 50/50 split. Your goals are aligned, but you are restricted on use of your assets.

A service-based publisher gets paid for ensuring that your book serves your goals such as getting speaking gigs, growing your client base or creating influence. A royalty-based publisher is incentivised to focus on selling copies of books, irrespective of your business goals.

My publishing company, Intellectual Perspective Press, is set up as a service-based publisher, with a 20% honour system reverse royalties payment. You get full rights to your assets, but I'm incentivised to make sure you look great so you sell books. I believe it's the best model to give you control of your sales and marketing, to use your book in whatever way works for you, and for us to grow a lovely long-term relationship.

Table of publishing models

Your publishing routes	Traditional publishing	Hybrid publishing	Self publishing	IPP*
Who's in control?	Them!	Joint usually	You	We're in it together
Who pays?	They do upfront, you do in the long term	You do, for professional services & ongoing with royalties	You for everything	You for the program, then you keep the royalties
Who wins?	You become a badly paid sales person for a multi-national	You both should, but it depends on their ethics	You, maybe, depends if you got good professionals	You!
Who does all the work?	You do the writing, they do the production & distribution	You do the writing, they do the production & distribution	You do the writing, production & distribution (unless you use professionals)	You do the writing with regular feedback. Professionals do everything else
Who does the marketing?	You!	What's marketing? Did you pay for it?	You!	We're in it together

* Intellectual Perspective Press

If you have self-published your book you are in control; you know what your costs to print one book are. You'll be able to make decisions on which of these tactics are going to work and you'll be able to change the tactic quickly. Yet another great reason for choosing yourself.

Your options may be restricted. Contact your publishing partner to find out what you can and can't do with your book. In the best case you have the following assets that you can use:

- Printed paperback book
- Printed hardback book
- Full colour PDF of the book
- Kindle version
- Audio version
- Book cover images (including 3D and placement)

With all of these assets to choose from (depending on your publishing route) you have more options than at first glance.

It's all about the process

I'm going to show you four strategies for getting books into the hands of the people who need them, and giving your book a job to do in your business. I have a favourite, but I use all of them at different times, depending on the job to be done for the book, the publishing route selected (which impacts the available options) and the appetite of the client to do the tasks.

Having a process is key. Shane Parrish of Farnham Street Blog[2], says: *"Amateurs have a goal. Professionals have a process."* In this book I'll layout the strategies and tactics, and explain the overall process so you can build your own unique process. The four main strategies we'll talk about are: One by one, one to many, strategically free and hyper-personalised.

One by one

One to many

Strategically free

Hyper-personalised

Irrespective of publishing route you have more options than you think, and have probably tried. You don't need to be flogging your book at the back of the room, begging on social media nor relying on one route to market.

We're going to look at the four strategies I recommend. But let's keep it as simple as possible. In order to get from the left-hand side (suspects and prospects, where you are paying) to the right-hand side (expects and referrers, where they are paying) you need to make an offer.

That offer is what we'll be talking about in the four strategies.

INCOMING
ATTENTION
(or re-attention)

OFFER

PAYOFF
MONEY or VALUE
EXCHANGE

Focus on the sales flow, moving from left to right, in a con-sidered and respectful way (not funnelling!):

1. Incoming: Get people's **attention**. Stop the scroll. Go where they are. If they're on LinkedIn be visible there. If they hang out at conferences, then get on the stage. If they're on your newsletter you have **information** about them (that they are interested in what you're saying), all you have to do is mes-sage them.

2. Offer: Make them an offer. Don't say only "buy my book" – make them an offer they can't refuse. We'll be looking at the four different types of offer in the next chapters. Your offer needs to focus on the value you bring, the problem you solve and the

cost to them of not getting the problem solved in a timely manner.

3. Payoff: Create a win-win value exchange. Frequently the value exchange is a solution to a problem in exchange for **money**, but that's not the only way you (as the author) can get value. You can get more information so you can make better business decisions, referrals because they **love** what you're doing so your business grows, or invitations to stages in front of bigger audiences.

> **The missing link between the left-hand side and the right is your offer. "Buy my book" is only one way of crossing the chasm.**

The five main attention attraction tactics for "Incoming" are:

1. Social media: You knew I was going to say it. Social media is a great way to see what people are talking about and then "do" things and "be" the person people come to when they have the problem you can solve.

2. Speaking gigs: Virtual webinars, real-life conferences, keynotes – your strategy of "speaking" in front of the right people and giving massive value so you attract attention.

3. Being a guest at or hosting your own "tables": I love creating and hosting groups of people with a common interest. You can run paid tables or free tables,

the key is to bring people together and break bread. You are then the centre of their attention.

4. Quizzes, diagnostics, self-tests: Everyone wants to know more about themselves and their business. This is a fast-growing way of getting attention and information.

5. Solve their first problem and be generous. Don't be overprotective about giving massive value for free to attract the right people. If you solve their first problem they will be more confident you can solve bigger problems.

> **Don't just get their attention – get their information and give them information. Information tactics such as a newsletter, webinars, diagnostics, and downloads help you solve the pains and problems of your prospects, and give you valuable information about them.**

Asset stacking

One of the problems authors have is focusing too much on just selling the book. I get it, I do it too. The desire to get people to make the jump from unknown suspect to delighted referrer is strong. And it can happen. You will get book reviews from people you have never met, and their reviews will influence more sales. This is just one strategy for your book.

It's more likely that you will need to provide a number of assets, or touchpoints, to get referring clients (and of course deliver an amazing book and service). I call this asset stacking, you use your assets to stack the odds in your favour and provide value for the reader (potential client).

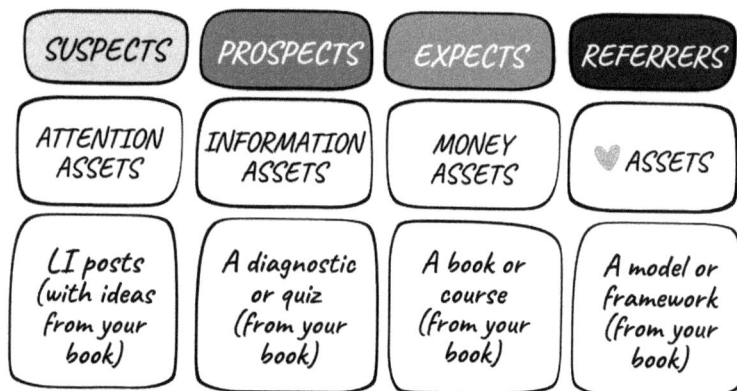

SUSPECTS	PROSPECTS	EXPECTS	REFERRERS
ATTENTION ASSETS	INFORMATION ASSETS	MONEY ASSETS	♥ ASSETS
LI posts (with ideas from your book)	A diagnostic or quiz (from your book)	A book or course (from your book)	A model or framework (from your book)

The people you want to attract and influence will be somewhere, such as on LinkedIn, on your newsletter, ex clients, colleagues. You need to get their attention or re-attention if you already know them. You provide valuable, transforming information that is actionable and helps them understand or solve their problem. They are so impressed they are happy to part with their cash when you make them an offer. This leads to a value exchange where you both get a payoff. They then go on to become happy clients and tell everyone how great you are. This is basic marketing 101.

> **Stop selling books – promote the transformation for your reader that your book promises.**

The great thing about a book is it can work at any of those stages in an asset stack. Your book is your most reliable, reusable and resourceful asset.

Endnotes

1.   You get 15% if you're lucky. Many publishing contracts are even lower.

3. WHAT YOU NEED TO KNOW BEFORE YOU START USING YOUR BUSINESS BOOK TO ATTRACT IDEAL CLIENTS ON AUTOPILOT – WITHOUT SHOUTING "BUY MY BOOK"

There are four strategies, and as we've already seen some will work for your book better than others depending on your publishing route and the job you want your book to do for you.

To keep it easy, we're going to use a simplified version of my AIM♥ marketing (Attention, Information, Money, Hearts) framework. The strategies we discuss will be the offer you make.

But before we can get started we need some basics.

Constraints, baby!

In marketing, constraints are essential because they encourage creativity and innovation. Limitations, whether they are in the form of budgetary restrictions, compliance rules or resource availability, force us to devise unique solutions. Don't view your constraints as obstacles, see them as opportunities (that's what your mom's always told you, right?). By facing and overcoming challenges, you can develop better strategies.

> **Constraints are good. Boundaries are essential.**

Selecting the right tactics depends on:

1. Them – the reader, potential client, actual client. Look at the Suspects, Prospects, Expects, Referrers diagram in chapter 2. If you are using your book to turn prospects into expects (buyers) then you won't want to use the "strategically free strategy" (strategy three).

2. You – what's your most wanted response from the tactic? Are you trying to grow your revenue? Then selling books one by one (strategy one) is a slow way to get there. Are you using your book to educate prospects so they become informed buyers, saving time and money in the sales process? Then making them pay to be sold to is a bad tactic (avoid strategy one).

3. The book – who published it, and how much it costs you to give away. Some strategies are prohibited by traditional publishing contracts. Your ability to give books away might be limited, so strategy three won't work for you.

4. Your experience – you may find some strategies easy to fit into your daily routines; you'll be comfortable doing them. Others will require actions you haven't thought about (calling people on the phone) and technologies you've never used (setting up sales pages). How easy it is to get done will depend on your technical prowess, the access you have to technology and your opportunity to exploit the assets you have (whether you've done these tasks before).

5. Your budget in terms of time, money and resources – can you do it yourself? Should you do it? Do you need to pay? Do you have permission? Each strategy has time, money and resource implications.

6. Expected impact – some tactics have a better chance of success than others: usually the ones we have most control over. How successful do you think the strategy will be? We both know marketing can't guarantee a result, but we can do tests and experiments to see how successful a tactic will be.

7. Time to outcome and results – some of the activities have a slow boil – they need a long-term mindset. Others have a delay from start to impact. You

may decide to start the long-term activities sooner so you get the results.

8. Your current position (where you're starting from, available assets for upsell) and your desired position (sell your business or grow your business?). You also have an A to B transformation for you or your business.

9. Your appetite for risk – the inherent riskiness causes some people to pull away from strategy three (giving your book away for free), especially traditionally published authors whose costs per book are higher. It's interesting to note that both high- and low-risk strategies are good.[3]

10. Joy, enthusiasm, fun. If you're not having fun, what are you having? Seriously, some of these strategies are much more fun than others (see strategy four, "hyper-personalised").

These questions are what stop most authors from getting started on marketing their book. What do you do first? Then what? I have a simple Selection Framework tool that might help you decide between multiple options, and put them into an order of action and a Book Marketing Canvas(tm) for you to capture all your decisions..

Get your own copy of The Selection Framework (also known as The Decision Thingy) in google sheets. Make a copy, edit your own ideas, calculate your score and then just select one. You can get all of the bonuses at www.shortvaluablebooks.com

You will also need to evaluate the time money and resources in a little more detail. Scribble in this book, or get a copy of the Book Marketing Canvas.

Time, money, resources

	Set up	See results	Manage
Time			
Money			
Resources			

> **The number one reason for authors not marketing, selling and using their book effectively is overwhelm. Break the overwhelm with constraints.**

The reasons for overwhelm can be summarised as:

1. Not knowing the job your book has to do, so you think it has to do everything or nothing.
2. Not knowing where your book works in the communications flow (Suspects, Prospects, Expects, Referrers).
3. Copying what other people are doing in a flurry of FOMO. Stop it – they haven't got a clue either.

Even after doing some logical evaluation by using the Selection Framework you might still feel stuck – how do you select the *right* strategy and tactic?

My advice?

Just pick one.

Your favourite. The easiest. Throw a dart at a piece of paper.

Then do it with energy and enthusiasm. You'll be ahead of 90% of authors.

> **Don't get overexcited and run paid ads into a strategy until you've proven the technology works, the book does the job it's supposed to do and you can handle the influx. Then hire someone to do it for you. You're not an (m)ad man – don't give yourself a new job to do.**

Automate, outsource, AI, oh my!

Most authors when thinking about this marketing malarky consider the three usual suspects options that can cause even more problems.

1. Do it yourself. You think a book is like other assets because it's physical, so you explain it, show it, flog it. It can't be that hard, can it? You're not selling it; you're "marketing" it. **The problem is people don't buy books. They buy solutions to problems.**

2. Pay someone a lot of money. Hire an agency, a PR or advertising company. Then when you run out of cash you end up complaining that books don't work. **Unless you know the job to be done how can you measure if it works?**

3. Do nothing. If you've written it, they will come. The publish and hope strategy I mentioned in chapter one. On the upside, at least you're not shouting "Buy my book!"

Options one and two can be mitigated for. Option three is a killer. For all of the four strategies I'm going to share I suggest you do it yourself first (with the help of experts), iron out the problems, test the variables. Then outsource or automate it.

> **Prove it first, then set up a flywheel.**

The flywheel concept, was introduced by Jim Collins in his book *Good to Great*[4]. It's a metaphor for a circular process where the momentum of successful efforts builds over time, eventually leading to a breakthrough result. Remind you of something? Our simmering pot of soup, the marketing hysteresis diagram.

Just like starting a flywheel or bringing a soup to simmer, marketing a book requires consistent efforts. Initial stages involve careful preparation. Next, as heat is consistently applied to the soup, you start promoting your book, but results may not be instant. This is like waiting for the soup to boil or the flywheel to gain momentum. Finally, when your book starts gaining recognition and sales (the soup is boiling or the flywheel spinning) the effort doesn't stop. You have to continue promoting, optimising, and engaging with your audience, like simmering the soup to perfection or keeping the flywheel in motion.

But you can't do it all yourself always. You shouldn't be the person chopping the veggies, stirring the soup, cleaning the pans. Yes, start the process, then automate or outsource.

Why? Because you are the talent, so do the things you are great at. That's thinking, writing, consulting, innovating, and speaking. My mentor, Piers Fallowfield-Cooper always asks: "What would you have to do if you were franchising your business or process?" Stop messing about with websites, technical headaches, and filling envelopes.[5]

Khe Hy[6] has a great diagram, The $10,000/hr work matrix, to help you visualise where your skills and leverage should be directed. Avoid the temptation of the delicious dopamine hits of getting $10/hour work completed (you know, the messing about in Canva, colouring in cells on the spreadsheet, obsessing over your Amazon ads) by outsourcing or automating. Learn how the strategy works, find the right people to help you, create the standard operations manual for the tactic then get out of the way.

> I'm growing a small team of professional strategic book coaches, launch and tactical coaches, editors and proofreaders. They have all been vetted by me, and trained in my strategies. If you need a hand I might have some to share.

You can only outsource or automate if you have a process or system (see I told you my engineering background would be useful). Why is a system crucial and what exactly does it entail? A system involves having a final target (the outcome) and interim checkpoints (the steps).

Lots of people set personal goals, like lead a healthier lifestyle, increase fitness, quit smoking, make more sales. I get it, I've set similar goals in the past too. However, I've discovered that not all goals are equally effective.

In his book, *Smart Change*, Dr Art Markman[7] makes a distinction between outcome goals and process goals. He explains that *"the most typical goal people pursue is an outcome goal. It refers to a specific state that you hope to reach in the future (like being a thin mother of the bride). The second type of goal is a process goal that focuses on a set of actions you can perform. As a side effect of those actions, you may achieve some desirable outcomes, but your focus is on the actions, not the outcome."* By following the steps, desired outcomes might be achieved, but the primary focus remains on the actions rather than the final result.

Think about the recent goals you've set. Were they outcome-oriented or process-oriented? Were you more focused on the end result or the journey to reach it? How successful were you in attaining your goal?

Outcome goals are bad news for us authors because:

1. We don't have control over the outcome. You can't force a person to buy from you (unless you've got a gun). The only aspect under your control is your own actions.

2. We encounter obstacles (which are inevitable) that discourage us. With an outcome goal, you might

be tempted to give up. However, with a process goal, you simply proceed to the next step.

3. Comparing your outcome on a particular day to someone else's can make you feel inadequate. However, comparing your actions to your own process goals can motivate you as you observe your progress incrementally.

4. If you're ruminating on an unachieved outcome goal, your thoughts can spiral into negativity and desperation (we've all been there, right?) By shifting your focus from the outcome to the process, you allow the results to take care of themselves.

When you have a process to follow (the four strategies) then you can keep your eye on the long-term destination. You stop turning the heat up and down, and work out how to get a steady simmer.

As Greg McKeown[8], one of my favourite authors says, *"Only once you give yourself permission to stop trying to do it all, to stop saying yes to everyone, can you make your highest contribution towards the things that really matter."*

Let's talk about the bots. You can't ignore them. It's better to be ahead of the game. You might not be ousted by a bot, but you might be shoved on your ass by a thought leader, consultant or founder using the bots. You can use AI (such as ChatGPT) to:

- Write book landing page and sales copy

- Rewrite your book description to make it shorter, longer, bulleted
- Repurpose whole chapters to turn into courses or articles
- Create marketing campaigns
- Write personalised emails
- Create your Amazon ads

In my book, *The DML Communications Compass*, I share some of my AI prompts. You can get the book (a free copy. I'm using strategy three with this book) and the prompts from www.shortvaluablebooks.com[9]

To get decent AI output you need great AI input – these are the prompts. If you put crap in, you will get crap out. **All AI output is a starting point not the finished item – AI creates drafts, not finished assets. You are the thinker.**

Finally, you might be tempted to hire yourself a marketing team. A marketing assistant costs anywhere from $30,000, only works the hours they turn up, needs feeding literally as well as with work to do, training, social support, etc. and there's no guarantee of successfully growing your business. Publishing your book and selecting one of the strategies outlined here to set up and put on automatic temperature control could grow your business exponentially. **Using your book as the marketing vehicle makes economical sense, if you actually *use* the book.**

It can cost less to publish a book and use it *as* your business marketing intern than it does to pay people to market and sell you.

Measure what matters to you (not the vanity metrics)

For a long time, driven by the traditional publishing industry, the measure of a good book was how long it had been on the bestseller list. Of course, that's a great metric and I'm sure James Clear and Tim Ferris are very happy with their long-term bestseller status. But there are only so many spaces at the top. If you measure your success by a metric that is outside your control you are destined to disappointment and despair.

Measure success by outcomes rather than inputs. Nobody gets wealthy by simply increasing their inputs (work). If you only ever get a single output or reward (say £500 or even £5,000) for a single input (like an hour of your time) then you're never going to get truly wealthy in your lifetime. Why not? Because as soon as you stop working the money stops coming in. When I talk about being wealthy I'm not talking about an arbitrary figure (you can choose whatever you like for that) I'm talking about being able to spend your time exactly as you wish. If you want to get this kind of wealth then you have to find ways to make a single input turn into multiple outcomes.

Writing a book is a good start because it requires just one input (I know there's lots involved!) but then it can keep bringing multiple outcomes (rewards by way of royalties and/or profits) indefinitely. View selling each book as a single input and then look at ways of getting multiple outcomes (rewards) from that one sale. That's by having a big back-end[10] that provides much more profit.

Set up your metrics based on the job your book has to do. If it's generating leads (suspects to prospects), how well did your book do? Do you need to adjust your strategy? Turn the heat up or down? The great thing about being in control of an asset like a book is that you get to turn on more clients at will.

> **You can control the leading numbers to influence the outcome. The lagging numbers are the score.**

What should you measure? Lagging and leading numbers. You're in control of the leading numbers – the things you do, the actions you take – and a spectator for the lagging – the results you achieved. Focusing too heavily on the lagging numbers (the outcome – books sold, clients converted) means you are at the mercy of factors outside your control. I talk about this in my book, *The Amazon Bestseller Plan*[11], an old book from 2006, which we used to sell for $49. We did all the leading numbers jobs, got the confirmation of buyers on the launch day, yet we were beaten by another, more famous book launching in the same week. We couldn't control their launch, only our actions. We were satisfied with our actions, the leading numbers. Yet we failed when counting the lagging numbers. You need the balance.

> **Stars aren't clients. Stop focusing on the Amazon stars, count the business outcomes.**

I started studying the stoics when my life had a bit of a wobble. I suddenly realised my control-freakery was not by best friend. Epictetus, a Greek Stoic philosopher, said: *"Some things are within our power, while others are not. Within our power are opinion, motivation, desire, aversion, and, in a word, whatever is of our own doing; not within our power are our body, our property, reputation, office, and, in a word, whatever is not of our own doing."*

You only have control over yourself

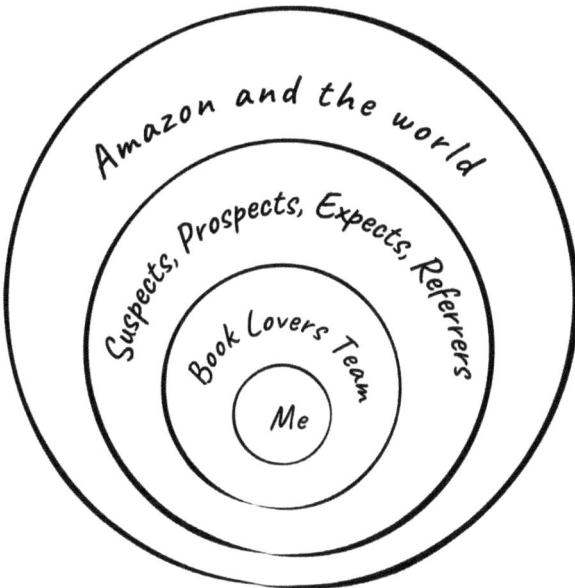

You cannot control the buyers, Amazon, not even your mom. You can only control (mostly) yourself and your own actions (you are your own doing, or undoing!) Measure your own actions and the results they bring.

What matters to you should be your actions in a marketing flow. On the left-hand side you are paying for the privilege, and on the right you are getting paid (in money and hearts).

INCOMING
ATTENTION
(or re-attention)

OFFER

PAYOFF
MONEY or VALUE
EXCHANGE

Decide what "growing your business" means to you and put numbers on it. I can't do that for you, but let's look at some figures. My clients range from solo business owners selling to other solo business owners, right up to founders and CEOs of major organisations, so I'm going to think of this as a scale. A new client for some authors will mean $10k income in one year. For another it could mean $100k. I'm not going to add the complication of lifetime value (though you should consider that too – homework for you); let's just play with getting one deal booked. And we'll assume (to help me with the maths) that the average is $50k.

In my business, the way I sell is through calls. People want to have a chat before they buy my main service. My book,

Stop writing books nobody reads, sits between the Suspects to Prospects stage and the Prospects to Expects stage, and I use it before and after discovery calls (see strategy four).

Now, answer the following questions for your business (and if you can't then go and find yourself a business coach who can help you with your business basics):

1. How many clients do you need to get overbooked[12] (or be a happy bunny) for your main business product or service? I need eleven per start date for the Publishing Cohort (ten spaces, plus one to overbook).

2. How many client calls (discovery calls or sales calls) do you need to make to get one new client for your main business offer? For example, I need to speak to three people to get one booked.[13] What are your numbers?

3. What's the time frame for consideration? If you're running a cohort or a launch, you need to work backwards from your live date. If you have a product or service that is a moving feast (always available) you will be able to make estimates based on previous "time from call to buy" data.

4. How many calls can you make in the time frame? I can do up to ten per week unless I hire a salesperson.[14]

5. How many books do you need to get out there to get those calls booked? Not every book will turn into a call.

6. What strategy will work best to get you your numbers?

Of course, you might not sell a product that requires a call. In strategy one, one by one, I show you how to use a sales flow (funnel) to get people to buy your self-serve course or product. If you sell SAAS or a product, then your numbers and process will be different. Strategy three, strategically free, might work really well for you.

When you know your numbers you can turn the heat up or down on your activity as part of the process. Let's look at the four strategies.

ENDNOTES

1. If you didn't write your book for a purpose with a clear job for it to do, go back to your basic book writing principles explained in: *Stop writing books nobody reads*.

2. The Difference Between Amateurs and Professionals: https://fs.blog/amateurs-professionals/

3. Nasim Taleb, in *The Black Swan: The Impact of the Highly Improbable*, talks about the barbell strategy, making sure that 90% of your capital is safe, by investing it in risk-free assets, and then investing the remaining 10% in very risky investments.

4. *Good to Great: Why Some Companies Make the Leap...and Others Don't*. Jim Collins, HarperBusiness (2001).

5. That was a note to self, that slipped into this book. This is a do as I say, not as I do moment. I truly wish I'd learnt the real art of delegation a long time ago. I'd be a millionaire by now.

6. You can see it on RadReads, The magic of doing $10,000 per hour work: https://radreads.co/10k-work/

7. *Smart Change: Five Tools to Create New and Sustainable Habits in Yourself and Others*, Dr Art Markman, TarcherPerigee; Reprint edition (January 6, 2015)

8. *He wrote two of my all time favourite books: Effortless: Make It Easier to Do What Matters Most and Essentialism: The Disciplined Pursuit of Less.*

9. You might be wondering why I'm giving so many great tools, canvasses and books away for free. It's because unless you come and register for the goodies I won't know who you are. If I don't know who you are I can't advance our relationship and create more valuable assets for you. See how it works?

10. I know, big back-end makes me giggle too. Yes, my back-end looks big in this.

11. *The Amazon Bestseller Plan*, written with my brother, Joe Gregory, isn't for sale any more – even though it's still really useful and relevant. You can get a PDF copy from me if you pop me a message.

12. A great book on this subject is, Oversubscribed: How to Get People Lining Up to Do Business with You by Daniel Priestley (Capstone, 2015).

13. That is a low conversion rate, yours might be much higher. My consideration time (how long before a client makes a decision) can be quite long for book coaching and publishing.

14. If you're reading this in 2023, I am looking for a salesperson – tell them to get in touch. If you're reading it later, what took you so long?

4. STRATEGY ONE: SELL YOUR BOOK ONE BY ONE – THE SLOW AND STEADY APPROACH

One by one

In the ever-evolving landscape of book marketing and selling, traditional routes remain influential. Platforms like Amazon and other online bookshops serve as reliable conduits, bridging the gap between your manuscript and the reader. These online platforms provide a global reach, connecting diverse readers to your work, regardless of geographical boundaries. Readers are confident in buying from Amazon; you really can't avoid them.

Wholesale routes to retail sales shouldn't be overlooked. Companies like Gardners and Ingram, as well as brick-and-mortar bookshops, offer a personal touch that many readers still enjoy. I love sniffing books (your own always smell best). The smell of fresh paper, the tangible weight of a book, the experience of browsing through physical aisles – these are all elements that a digital marketplace cannot replicate. It's less easy to ensure your book lands on the shelves of real book-shops, but it's a channel that is available to you irre-spective of your publishing route.

> **Most people plan to sell their book. It's a good tac-tic. Remember, it's not necessarily the book sale that might generate the revenue or advance the relation-ship. It's what you sell after selling the book that can increase the value of your business.**

This strategy – selling your book one by one – has been used to help authors like Mel Robbins, Brendon Burchard, and Tony Robbins expand their audiences, businesses and legacies. You know this is true because you've probably bought one of their books in the past.

Finally, never underestimate the power of translations and foreign rights. By translating your work and selling foreign rights, you can significantly broaden your book's audience. This approach ensures your ideas resonate not just within your home market, but also across different cultures and languages around the globe, thereby ampli-fying your book's influence and reach.

All strategies to get your book in the hands of readers have issues that need resolving. Let's have a look.

Problems (and solutions) of the sales strategy

All strategies have issues. The sales strategy, even though it's the most obvious, has some of the worst.

Problems with selling your book through the traditional routes:

1. It can be painfully slow. So slow you can't feel the heat rising. And that means you give up too soon.

2. You can sound like a demented energiser bunny, shouting "buy my book" to anyone who pauses long enough to hear you. You'll end up turning their ears off.

3. You don't know who bought the book, so you can't follow up. All your efforts go into book sales not business growth.

> The book is just a vehicle, an asset, a way of getting people to understand what you're telling them. Your value is in the critical thinking and simplifying of the concept that you did to write the book. Show them the solution to their problem.

Ways to make it easier on yourself (and the readers):

1. Stop being such an impatient pants. I have this same issue. I put my book out for sale and expect billions of sales in the first day. The one book at a time strategy can be slow. Keep your eye on the

process not the outcome (see chapter three), and you'll stop yourself from going completely bonkers.

2. Change the tune. **Stop selling the book, sell the solution to their problem.** Your book has a job to do; even if they don't *buy* the book, knowing that you know the answer to their problem means you are now under consideration. You don't need to shut up entirely, just sing a different song.

3. Unless you want to be a badly paid salesperson for your publisher and Amazon, just selling books isn't a great option. If you are in control of your book then make sure there are some enhancements available in the book to get readers to give you their name and email address. Then you can follow up with them. (You do have a follow-up strategy, don't you?) You will have seen these enhancements through-out this book. In fact the first real page was a request for you to contact me. If you bought this book from Amazon this is my way of finding out who you are. (I promise not to stalk you.)

> **Collect email addresses, then do something with them. Email addresses are not a business asset unless they are recent, relevant and regularly engaged.**

Already published your book and not getting sales?

Before we get into the mechanics of this strategy, one of the complaints I hear the most is that a book published a couple of years ago has stopped selling. If that's you, here are some quick questions. Answer honestly:

1. Do you still love your book?
2. Have you done everything you can with the asset(s) you've got?
3. Does your book have a job to do in your business?

It's normal to fall out of love with your book – but you need to work out why. If it's because it's just a sloppy shelf-sitter, then let's kick its ass and get it working for you. If it's because you or your business has changed, now might be the right time to think of how to rework the asset, get control back if you've relinquished any rights and recycle or upcycle your assets. If you do love your book, put a smile on your face and let people know about it. I'll show you how.

Your book isn't the pages it's written on – it's the ideas, the IP, the concept, the frameworks, the case stories, your stories. You constructed your book as you were writing, now might be the time to deconstruct the book and reuse those assets.

> **Don't talk about the book, talk about the transformation. Then all of the marketing materials you create will be reusable across any asset (print book, ebook, courses, interventions, speeches).**

Chris Fenning, author of two books, *The First Minute: How to Start Conversations That Get Results* and *Effective*

Emails: The Secret to Straightforward Communication at Work doesn't have that problem. Since 2020, *The First Minute* has sold over 30,000 copies, won awards and has more than 500 ratings on Amazon. His book is incredibly specific and solves a valuable problem.

He runs Amazon adverts because he knows his book generates business. Chris: *Without Amazon ads, I would not have sold so many books. Plain and simple. I know that for every 1,000 books I sell, I will get a corporate or personal client and that's worth a lot more than a book sale. I spend thousands per month on ads.*

Running Amazon ads to your book will also help with organic sales, due to the boost in the sales ranking. Chris has a series of books that he will add to in the future (a great tactic, I talk about it in tactic 1, later in this chapter) and running adverts to one book usually boosts sales of your other books.

> **The economics of running ads (Amazon, LinkedIn, Facebook, etc) to your book might not stack up if you are traditionally or hybrid published. Unless you have a solid process for turning readers into higher priced clients, your book is frequently a loss leader or (hopefully) a break-even marketing asset in your business marketing stack.**

If your book is only available in print, could you do an ebook version? Or an audio book? Or a YouTube series? The more book assets you have the easier your job will be.

And talking of jobs, if your book doesn't have a job to do (go and look at the Suspects, Prospects, Expects, Referrers model earlier), how are you measuring its success? If your book's job was to generate leads (Prospects in my model), how many has it created? How have you set it up to succeed in its job?

Book selling tactics

I'm not going to go into the 1,001 ways of selling your book. There are other books out there that will overwhelm you with tactics. Most of them are useful, but the volume will make your eyes bleed.

You don't only have to sell your book on Amazon or in bookshops. You can set up book sales flows where you take a version of your book (ebook, PDF, audio, print) and use it to get attention, make an offer and create a powerful payoff.

> **You can sell direct from your own website too. It's not only Amazon that sells books.**

You can sell directly from your own website, so you have the buyer data. I don't recommend this option unless you have a lot of fingerfall[1] at your site (or a plan to get fingerfall) and a web development team to make sure the process is smooth and safe. Derek Sivers does have a lot of traction on his site, and sells books directly. Derek mentioned in an email: *"When you buy my books directly from me, all the profits go to a life-saving charity. $575,000 donated so far, including another $100K this week. See* *https://sive.rs/575k So if you were thinking of buying my books (audiobook/ebook/paper/etc.) or gifting them to others, please do it directly."*

If in doubt sell where the fingerfall of readers is already established – Amazon, Google, Goodreads etc. **If you have the appetite for selling your book from your own website then these two tactics are fab.**

> **When you've proven this tactic works for you, you can run adverts to your offer page and turn the heat up on your incoming prospects to increase the fingerfall. Don't spend money on adverts until you're sure it works.**

1. Low-cost book bundle

As with all these strategies, your incoming attention seeking needs to be appropriate to the people you are trying to influence. Let's assume you've written an article on LinkedIn and your desire is to turn Suspects (people you think might want the solution you offer) into Expects (clients who have paid to get the expectation of relief from their problem). The offer you make (that bridges the gap) could be a bundle of all your book assets.

> **If you don't have the appetite for taking money from your website, let them buy the print book from Amazon, ask them for their receipt and contact details, and then immediately send them the audio and ebook, so they get instant satisfaction. And you get their email details.**

You can add in other items to your offer, such as courses, webinars, events, membership, downloads. What you bundle is up to you. Set your price to make it an easy decision for the buyer. Your payoff will be new people on your list who have indicated, **with their cash**, that they are interested in what you're doing. You can then nurture them with your mailing list and sell them other books, more expensive products, done for you services, done with you services, etc.

This isn't a new tactic. The low cost book bundle has been around a while. For example, the "One Book Millions Method" concept, as presented in the book of the same name, is a scalable and predictable marketing strategy. With a low cost book bundle you can build trust and authority while adding a high volume of new clients to your business, and then turn them into clients for coaching programmes, services and digital courses.

> **Remember to ask for a book review. This is your best way of getting organic sales.**

The price doesn't even have to be that "low", and the book doesn't have to be printed. Steph Smith sells her ebook, "Doing Content Right" for $150[2]. She sells a bundle of 270 page ebook in multi formats, and you get access to her creator community, videos and audio sessions. More than 3400 people have bought Steph's book bundle.

> **Want to know what the best bundle is? A bundle of your own books.**

Write another book (series-ly). There are massive benefits to writing more books: you can develop your ideas, delve deeper, speak to a different reader, share new ideas, respond to new technologies or techniques etc. Amazon also rewards series of books by showing them together – if a reader buys one book in your series, they will see the other books and might even buy them.

You don't even need to have the whole series in print. Professor Andy Pardoe[3] has a series of books about AI, they are all in Kindle, they are not print books. Yuval Noah Harari is a great example of an author using the power of a series. He finished his first book (in the A Brief History Series), *Sapiens: A Brief History of Humankind* in 2015.The next book, *Homo Deus: A Brief History of Tomorrow* in 2017. He now sells both as a series. He also upcycled his books into graphical books for (big) kids and produced both books as a separate series.

When you have a series of books you can create the best bundle – your valuable assets – and demand a higher price.

2. Book plus upsell

You don't have to wait to ask for the upsell (the previous tactic). You can ask for it during the sales process. This is trickier to set up, and requires you to have the other assets already created (such as a course or webinar); however, it is a fast way to increase the payoff.

This is a sales funnel, or as I prefer to call it, a sales flow. Despite my distaste for the term "funnel", I appreciate the essence of this concept. The sales flow captures the journey of turning a potential reader into a loyal customer. It's a strategy that nurtures the relationship with the reader, gradually leading them from awareness to purchase, getting them on your list so you can sell more solutions in the future, and eventually, helping them become referrers of your book and your work.

"Automatic Clients" is an approach detailed in an ebook by Robert Neckelius. The book's premise is to help readers turn inexpensive ebook sales, around $5–$19, into much larger transactions, upwards of $5,000. This business model involves getting attention by selling a cheap ebook, and during the sales process they offer more options to make your life easier (a video course or swipe files that get you the result faster). The by-product is getting people on your list, so you can convert those customers into larger sales later on.

The upsells need to be urgent and appropriate. Don't just shove any old course into the flow. You need to help the reader get their pain resolved faster, easier or cheaper. You do this with the Cialdini principles of persuasion[4].

Robert Cialdini's principles of persuasion can be applied effectively to the marketing and sale of business books. Here's a quick review of these principles in relation to the book plus upsell tactic:

1. Reciprocity: By providing some valuable content or insights for low cost, you can create a sense of

obligation in readers, which may make them more likely to purchase higher priced items during the sales flow.

2. Scarcity: Create a sense of urgency or exclusivity about the offer (e.g. limited edition, time-sensitive bonuses) to increase perceived value and motivate purchases.

3. Authority: Your credentials, endorsements from other respected figures, or demonstrating your deep knowledge on the topic can increase the book's credibility and persuade potential buyers.

4. Consistency: Because they have already bought your book, they are more likely to purchase the other offers to maintain consistency with their past behaviour.

5. Liking: People are more likely to buy from authors they like, so establishing a personal connection with potential readers can be beneficial. Adding a video helps so they can see you in action.

6. Social Proof: Testimonials, reviews, and endorsements can show potential buyers that others have found value in the book bundle, increasing its appeal.

These tactics can be used in all your marketing efforts. In this case you could make an upsell offer that is only available to the next 100 buyers, and they need to get it now. Show happy people (real faces are best) and how they've used your products or services to solve their problem.

> The limited edition tactic can work for more than your bonuses. If you are self-published or have published with us, creating a limited edition version with extra information, or a hardback version is a simple process that generates attention.

Perhaps the most fearless "one by one" tactic I've seen is from my friend and mentor, Filip Fučić. With consultant Claus Raasted, he wrote: *PRICING EXPERTISE: How to get paid what you deserve by clients who deserve you*[5]. They explain that they're not selling a book, even though it is book-shaped, and for that reason they haven't priced it like a book. They've priced it on the value you get for the problem they solve. Filip: *And since we wanted to practice what we preach, it made no sense to base its price on the costs of our time, printing, shipping, illustrating, or whatever. Nobody buys a book because it has 218 pages.*

Whether you buy the hardcover, the digital copy, or both you pay $560. They also offer a 100% money back guarantee to remove the concern of it being a gimmick. The book is essentially a beautifully illustrated, condensed version of a pricing course. They are selling their book for $560, not to make sales of the book, but to get attention from people who should be interested in pricing strategies.

Filip and Claus might not sell thousands of copies (the usual measure of success), but those people who do buy turn into educated, informed and enthusiastic clients.

Filip and Claus have reduced the time (save time/money) taken to bring a client into their world, generated substantial revenue on the first sale, and taken people from suspects to expects and then referrers with one asset. It's now much easier for them to sell a higher priced product.

You can turn the heat up on this type of strategy by buying adverts on Facebook, Google or LinkedIn. But before you do that make sure your book is attracting the right people, and you have the upsell to the next more expensive product or service ready to go. This could be one-to-one, an event or a course. With all advertising start slow and low, run tests, ramp up when you prove your flow. And get help if you've never done this before. It's easy to waste a lot of money quickly.

> I have a **Notion database of images of book sales pages that show all of the strategies I'm sharing in this book. I share them with my clients for inspiration. If you'd like to get a look at it just pop to www.shortvaluablebooks.com**

Remember, you can sell your book through more channels than the online bookshops. You will need to get some technical help, but once the process is set up and proven you can turn the heat up at will.

ENDNOTES

1. It's like footfall, but for fingers. I might have made that word up. I make up at least one word per book.

2. Steph Smith, https://doingcontentright.com/

3. *Unlimited AI Strategy for Business Growth: A Guide for Entrepreneurs and SME Owners* (It's All One's & Zero's), Andy Pardoe, self-published.

4. *Influence: The Psychology of Persuasion*, Robert B. Cialdini, Harper Business. I actually have three copies, that's how persuasive he is.

5. You can get your copy here: https://fearless-pricing.com/

5. STRATEGY TWO: MOVE YOUR BOOK ONE TO MANY – EXPANDING YOUR REACH THROUGH COLLABORATION TO GET YOUR BOOK IN FRONT OF MULTITUDES

One to many

Harnessing the power of collective effort, shared resources and broad networks can significantly propel your book's visibility. Strategy two – one to many – operates on the principle of amplifying your reach without necessarily expending your own resources, or in other words, not using your own gas.

In the vast world of publishing, collaboration becomes a potent tool, bringing the advantages of others' resources into play – their money, time and networks. The essence of this approach lies in forging partnerships, actively participating in events and connecting with corporations. Engaging these people (people run all of these activities, real human beings) not only broadens your potential readership but also promotes your book in places beyond your personal reach.

Here's a thought that might surprise you: selling 100 books could be as straightforward as selling just one. Sounds paradoxical? However, once your book reaches the right platforms, where like-minded people gather or corporations seek valuable content, your single sale can multiply exponentially. This is a true wholesale channel, that you can enthusiastically pursue.

Remember this – at its core, your book is a vehicle to transformation. It carries ideas, insights and inspirations that can instigate change in the reader. This transformative power is what people buy, not just the pages bound together. Your task, as an author, is to ensure that this vehicle reaches as many people as possible, paving the way for countless transformations.

> **Your book is a vehicle to a transformation. People buy transformations, not books.**

Problems (and solutions) of the one to many strategy

While the one to many strategy can be effective, there are three major challenges that can hinder its success:

1. Identifying the right partners: This strategy heavily relies on partnering with individuals or organisations

that have the reach you want. However, finding partners who align with your book's theme, audience and overall goals can be difficult. Misaligned partnerships can dilute your brand and lead to wasted efforts.

2. High dependence on external entities: The one to many strategy can leave you dependent on others for the promotion and distribution of your book. This may lead to uncertainty and lack of control over how your work is presented or marketed, and there's always a risk that they may not fulfil their part of the agreement. Remember our stoic circles in chapter three? You are ceding control, make sure you're ready for it!

3. Quality control and consistency: When you rely on other people, maintaining the quality and consistency of your book's presentation can be challenging. Different organisations may interpret and convey your work's messages differently, which could lead to inconsistencies in how your book is seen by your audience.

> **You need other people. This means you need to be "useful" to them.**

To fix the three major challenges associated with the one to many strategy:

1. Invest time in comprehensive research to identify the right partners. Look for organisations or individuals that share a similar target audience and more important, values that will strengthen your

book's promotion. Try networking events, forums and conferences within your area to find potential partners. Don't only look for the biggest, look for the most aligned with you and your ideas.

2. Mitigate dependency, establish clear agreements and expectations with partners at the outset. I know you're lovely, but please, get a contract in place. Ensure the contract includes the scope of their involvement, timelines and outcomes. Regular communication can also help create a mutually beneficial relationship.

3. Maintain consistency in your book's presentation, create a detailed guide for your partners that out-lines key messages, branding and communication style. Regularly review what they're saying about your book and provide constructive feedback. Your lexicon will be invaluable here. If you don't have a lexicon have a read of **Stop writing books nobody reads**, for why a lexicon is important.

Inventing another chicken and egg problem

I frequently hear from potential authors (especially if they want to get traditionally published) that they don't have a big enough platform. We all know we need a platform, a social media following, a newsletter, a Substack, a flourishing YouTube channel and all that jazz. With those numbers of buyers in place your book will sell easily.

If you had those high numbers in place you probably wouldn't be looking for a traditional publisher – they'd be looking for you.

This is the main issue you face when you're looking for partners to market your book. You want access to their network, they want access to something they don't have.

What else do you bring to the party?

To make yourself and your book valuable to third parties requires establishing the relevance of your book to *their* interests, providing them with something valuable, and showing the mutual benefits of the collaboration.

Clearly demonstrate how your book relates to the interests of potential partners. This could mean aligning with their brand, values or audience. For instance, if your book discusses leadership principles, it might be attractive to businesses, leadership coaches or management training programmes.

Provide something extra that's valuable, exclusive content, a percentage of sales made through their channels, or free workshops or webinars that might interest their audience.

Shine the spotlight on them, not the book. Make them the star of the partnership deal. Interview them, get them on your podcast, share their work.

And show them the benefits of co-promotion. Make it clear how promoting your book can enhance their brand, reach a larger audience or provide unique content for their followers.

Remember, partnerships work best when they're mutually beneficial. Always consider what you're offering them, not just what they can do for you.

Other people's networks, time and money tactics

Leveraging other people's networks (OPN), time (OPT) and money (OPM) involves strategic partnerships, collaborations and mutual value exchange, serving as a potent tactic for enhancing your reach, saving resources and driving success.

3. Partnerships

Rather than spending money on advertising or exhausting your own networks, you can use other people's time, money or networks by partnering.

This can work by getting together with a group of business people who all serve the same audience. You all offer your books as a book bundle and receive the contact details of everybody who signs up.

I did this in 2022. I was a summit speaker. I gave away my book and people got added to my list. It's a good tactic if you run the partnership as you get yourself in front of everybody's audience. However, organising it is a pain in the ass.

For the first time, get yourself on somebody else's conference or summit, see how it works, and then consider running your own version.

The partnership route also works if you're exhibiting or speaking at an in-person conference or event. Instead of asking for a speaking fee you can get your book in the goody bags. If you're a professional speaker you get paid for speaking, don't drop your fee. If you're an unprofessional speaker (you know what I mean) this is a great way for speaking agents and bookers to get to test you, while you get your book to their audience.

You can find partnership deals from your current lists or asking for referrals. You might even find partners in your town or village. In 2014, I compiled and wrote a recipe book in English and Spanish, with the wonderful women (and one man) from my village in Spain. The book, *Spanish Village Cooking - Recetas del Campo*, was a bestseller on Amazon and we sold over 2,000 copies locally. A mighty feat for a village of 101 people, and a great example of the power of partnerships and OPN. All proceeds went to the village fiesta, we had a seven day party.

Another great way of finding partners is to be part of a writing cohort. Our book publishing cohort means that not only do you think, write and publish together, you also help one another in the future. You will make great connections, friendships and partnerships during the process. At launch you will all launch together, getting over any nervousness or imposter syndrome. Your cohort will get to understand you and your book, they will want to partner with you in the future too. You don't have to do this alone.

> **Don't only think online, your book could be a great upsell where footfall of your target audience passes. If your book is about getting fit, then gyms could be a great place to have a book display.**

Ann Latham, a long time client and friend, and the Queen of Clarity has used this tactic. Ann has self-published some books, been traditionally published by Bloomsbury, and was one of our first Cohort Publishing authors. Her book, *The Disconnect Principle: Eliminate difficult conversations with clarity and empathy*[1] came out in November, 2022 and was an instant Amazon bestseller. In 2023, she was approached by a colleague to create a workbook to accompany the main book for an adjacent audience. Of course, there was some work involved to create a valuable asset, but the investment opens up a new market and reuses the main book asset. This is an audience Ann would have been unlikely to reach by other means. By partnering with an expert in a different niche, Ann has opened up more sales opportunities and created a new asset.

4. Sponsors

Getting a sponsor for your book is an amazing way of getting credibility clues.

A sponsor endorses your book and pays to have copies available to their following. This is an excellent other people's network, time and money strategy.

One of my writing clients, a sales trainer in the auto industry, did a great sponsorship deal with a magazine. The industry leading magazine publisher bought and bundled over 2,000 copies of his book, slipping them into the plastic bag before sending them to subscribers. This got the author in front of decision makers in his industry. As we know, most normal sane people don't throw books away, so even now he gets comments from old clients and new about the book still sitting on their desk.

The beauty of this strategy was that his book got in front of a large targeted audience, and even if the recipients were already his clients, he got a credibility boost because he had been selected by the industry leader (the magazine publisher).

> **Sponsorship deals get you in front of large audiences. You get a credibility clue because you've been selected by an industry leader.**

If your book is self-published or with a hybrid publisher, you will almost certainly be able to do a special edition for sponsored books. Make it exclusive:

- Change the cover to include the sponsor's branding or logo
- Add a special edition foreword from the sponsor
- Add a new call to action page, specifically speaking to the new target audience

If you get a sponsorship opportunity make the most of it.

Where should you look for sponsorship deals?

- Ask your clients and contacts
- Organisations and groups that attract your audience (remember, go where the readers are)

- Magazines, newspapers, periodicals that cater to your geographic or industry sector
- Event and conference organisers
- When you are doing a speaking gig or workshop
- Corporations and larger businesses

The other side of sponsorship deals is when *you* pay to sponsor. Unless you get a great deal, have seen success with sponsoring previously or have deep pockets I suggest you **focus on getting them to sponsor you** (an edition of your book).

> **If you have self-published or been cohort published with me, then you can do a personalised branded edition of your book just for the sponsor.**

The one to many strategy is frequently overlooked because it appears to be too difficult. Just switch your thinking to selling your book to one person in a large organisation so they can sell to many for you.

ENDNOTES

1. Ann Latham, *The Disconnect Principle: Eliminate difficult conversations with clarity and empathy*, Intellectual Perspective Press, 2022.

6. STRATEGY THREE: THE ART OF GIVING – LEVERAGING "FREE" AS A STRATEGIC TOOL (NOT AS EASY AS IT SOUNDS)

Strategically free

You might be tempted to think that giving away your hard-earned creation – your book – is a sure-fire way to attract readers. In theory, it sounds simple, like a straight-forward transaction. The reality, however, is considerably more complex. The process of offering your book for free, enticing as it may sound, is not as easy as it appears on the surface.

> It's much harder than it sounds to give people things.

Consider, for example, the idea of the free PDF, once the golden standard of lead magnets. This strategy has seen its effectiveness diminished over time, mainly due to oversaturation and the subsequent devaluation of ebooks (frequently poorly written, barely credible, often thinly concealed sales brochures). Free information is no longer scarce, and a free PDF is often met with scepticism rather than excitement.

The strategic use of "free" is a legitimate marketing strategy, when used judiciously. It can create buzz, build an audience and establish you as an authority in your field. However, it is essential to remember that "free" does not mean "without value". Your work has value, and giving it away for free should be a strategic decision aimed at enhancing that value, not undermining it.

> **Free is a legitimate strategy, when used well.**

Problems (and solutions) of the free strategy

It might seem paradoxical, but giving people things can be a challenging job. Offering something for free often comes with its own set of hurdles, from creating awareness and interest to dealing with logistical issues. Nonetheless, if navigated correctly it can be rewarding, leading to an expanded reader base and a stronger bond with your audience.

> **Your writing journey, like any other, is filled with strategic decisions. To give or not to give? That is the question.**

Problems of giving books away for free

1. It's really not easy to give things away for free. I've seen you dodging the Hari Krishnas at the airport – you know if you take something for free there must be a catch. If Cialdini taught us anything it was not to take free things from strangers (he also taught us how we can use that to our advantage).

2. People tend to devalue a free thing and get it just because it's free. They might not be a great fit for you or your business, but they didn't want to miss out on the free book!

3. You end up with a database of freebie seeking, curious tyre kickers (or your competitors).

Curious, desperate, inspired: As you're growing your business using your book to generate leads you will start to notice that not all leads are created equal. I wrote about this in the first book I ever wrote (with my brother, Joe Gregory), *The Gorillas Want Bananas*, in 2003[1]. Even though these are massive generalisations (sorry, not sorry) it's more important now than ever as the market is flooded with options.

Curious people have probably spoken to your competitors, read all the books on the subject, and had plenty of discovery calls. They are frequently lovely people who are genuinely interested in what you're doing, but they're unlikely to buy from you (or in fact anyone). They are, however, great at making referrals, so ask them to write that review and tell people how great your book is.

Desperate people will buy your book, course, pro-gramme and you when they have exhausted all other options. They leave everything until the last minute then expect miracles. They are the most critical, and they're never satisfied. They will always associate you with their desperation. Avoid them or put your prices up really high.

Inspired people will buy what you're selling to solve the problem they have. You won't need to wait for long until your free book turns into a happy client.

> **The problem with free books is that it attracts curi-ous and desperate people. Give them more free stuff, ask them to refer you and then put your prices up.**

Ways to overcome the free book problems

1. The act of giving a book away for free aligns with Cialdini's Principle of Reciprocity, which says that people naturally want to return a favour when they receive something. A free book creates a sense of indebtedness in the recipient, who may feel com-pelled to reciprocate. They might share the book with others, tell everyone about your work, or go on to buy other things from you.

2. Put a quiz in front of the free book. That way they have "worked" for the book and you get data. When people work for a free book they feel more inclined to read it, refer it and take action on the information.

3. Your job as chief marketer and bottle washer is to convert curious people to buyers. You need a follow-up plan. Have a way for curious people to keep diving into your stuff until your energy and enthusiasm inspire them to do business with you.

> **Make people do a little work or pay a small amount to get your free book, that way they will value it more.**

There's plenty of evidence to show that people value free stuff more if they "pay" for it.

There's the mere ownership effect[2], the phenomenon that people tend to value things more just because they own them. This has been shown in a number of studies, including one where people were given a coffee mug and then asked how much they would be willing to sell it for. Those who had earned the mug by completing a task valued it more than those who had simply been given it[3]. There's also the endowment effect where people place a higher value on things that they own, even if they have no intention of using them.

Of course, we want people to read our books, do what we suggest and get the result we promise, so just owning the book isn't enough. **The beauty of the strategically free tactics is that you get their email address, and with your follow up you can encourage the transformation.**

Why modelling other authors can backfire

I see this problem mostly in the free books category. You spot another, successful business owner giving their books away. They are successful; it must be because of the free books, right? Maybe. Free books tactics are the tiny tip of the gigantic iceberg. You can't see what's below the waterline, but it's big. Copying their visible tactic can lead to ruin.

Watching and learning is a great idea. I have a database of book sales pages and launch pages for inspiration. You can get a copy of it if you want from www.shortvaluablebooks.com But, I always have a plan – I know what my below the waterline looks like.

Daniel Priestley, founder of Dent, is well known for giving away his books. *But he isn't doing it only for altruistic* reasons. He has a follow-up plan; the books are part of a thought-out strategy. To get a book you have to provide details – sometimes quite a few details. And he's almost always pulling you into a sales flow (funnel). His most recent book is the clearest example of this. Everybody is talking about diagnostics and quizzes as a great marketing tool, and Daniel's company ScoreApp is a leader in the field. It's no surprise that Daniel wants to educate a large audience with his book, *Scorecard Marketing: The four-step playbook for getting better leads and bigger profits*[4], when the upsell is a SAAS product at $39 per month. It's a smart, well considered tactic.

Some people you might model (copy) might not even have a strategy. Or the strategy could be a copy of someone else's... The funhouse hall of mirrors is alive and well in book marketing.

Free book tactics

If you have a proprietary model or system your book can be an ambassador and educator. Your book can save you money and time by educating people about your process. It can increase the value of your business by getting new Suspects to put their hands up and become Prospects, adding themselves to your mailing list.

The free book strategy taps into the Cialdini Principle of Commitment, as those who accept your free book are more likely to align their future actions with their commitment, which may involve engaging more deeply with your work. The seemingly simple act of giving a book away for free leverages psychological principles to encourage engagement and loyalty among readers.

5. Free ebook

When we write a book we don't end up with just the physical printed copies. Most authors will have at least three assets that you can use in different ways. The free ebook strategy takes advantage of one of the assets – the PDF or Kindle version (.mobi). This all depends on your publishing model. Some traditional publishers do not allow you to give your book away for free in fear of cannibalising printed book sales. I've found the opposite is true – real fans want your book in all the formats useful to them. After receiving a free PDF they may go on to buy a printed copy or an audio book.

You first need to get their attention in a noisy marketplace. Let's say you've done an event or a podcast. You can make an offer of a free ebook, and all they have to do is give you their details. They get the free book and you get their details.

> **The free ebook strategy removes one of the main challenges of selling through retailers like Amazon: you don't know who bought the book. This is one of the best ways of getting data about who's bought your book so that you can communicate with them in the future.**

You get them on your list, and they become prospects because they put their hand up.

With the strategically free strategies it's all in the follow up. Have a system in place for emailing them after a short period of time (give them a week to read it) and ask for their feedback. Suggest they read certain chapters, message them with the page number. You want your free book to be read, not forgotten. People don't buy more services nor refer you if they haven't read your book.

> **Ask for a review. If your book is also available on Amazon ask for a review there, or on Goodreads. If not, ask for an endorsement on LinkedIn.**

Of course, you can just give it away as a PDF after they fill in their details (name and email address). My favourite way is to get them to answer three questions so you get a bit more data. You may ask for their title, how big their business is, what's their most pressing problem. Whatever it is that you want to know. They answer the questions and get the payoff.

> Another way to get their attention is to make the offer of a free book after someone has read an article on your website. You can pop up the offer as a tactic to keep their attention for just a little longer and to get them on your list. Have I mentioned you want to get people on your list?

Another paradigm shift in the "free" strategy is to give your physical, print book away entirely free to anyone who signs up, as advocated by Daniel Priestley. This strategy requires not just a belief in the power of "free" but also a genuine desire to spread one's ideas, understanding that value can be extracted from places other than the cover price. Dent have given away tens of thousands of books and it works really well for them.

> Getting your book into people's hands is good. That's our goal.

6. Free book plus shipping

One increasingly popular strategy circumvents the issue of free being undervalued by providing a physical book for free, and asking only for postage and packaging fees. This approach offers a tangible value – a physical book feels "real" in a way a digital download does not, providing a higher perceived value to the potential reader – and they have skin in the game because they've paid for shipping.

This is a great tactic for people who are already on your mailing list. They get a free printed book and they only have to pay shipping. You've probably seen this one; it's one of the favourite tactics that's going around at the moment. And it works really well. This was Hormozi's tactic in his Guinness Book of Records beating book launch. For me, the sour taste was in the cost of shipping. He blamed the shipping companies, but that seemed like an excuse (it also took more than a month to arrive, fortunately it was worth the wait).

You set up a page on your website with the offer of a free book, with $7.99 post and package costs. You would have to buy stock of your book (easy if you've self-published) and be prepared to post copies out as the orders come in. You can of course send directly from Amazon, but do the maths to work out your costs. You can use a dropshipping company, such as BookVault (see the PS chapter at the end), to automate this process too.

Get help with the technical parts of the setup, especially for physical product shipping.

It might be more cost effective to buy 100 books at a time yourself and then send them out with a hand-written note in a nice pretty envelope (see strategy four for special package magic).

The other benefit to you, the owner of the book, the owner of the asset, is you've now got their mailing address, extra data and more information.

But the biggest benefit is they are on your list and they have already demonstrated purchase intent. They've already given you some cash. They're a more interesting potential client. They've moved beyond interested to inspired.

ENDNOTES

1. *The Gorillas Want Bananas:* The Lean Marketing Handbook for Small Expert Businesses, Debbie Jenkins and Joe Gregory, Bookshaker, 2003

2. Kahneman, D., Knetsch, J. L., & Thaler, R. H. (1990). Experimental tests of the endowment effect. Journal of Economic Perspectives, 5(1), 193-206.

3. Soman, D. (1998). The influence of ownership on valuation: The endowment effect revisited. Journal of Behavioral Decision Making, 11(1), 57-66.

4. *Scorecard Marketing: The four-step playbook for getting better leads and bigger profits,* Daniel Priestley, Rethink Press 2022

7. STRATEGY FOUR: ONE REAL PERSON PER DAY – HYPER-PERSONALISED, EXPECTED, REFERRED

Hyper-personalised

Every day, our paths intersect with hundreds of people, both virtually and physically. We form impressions, make connections and continue with our lives. Yet, how many of these individuals do we genuinely see, understand and touch (not that kind!) in a meaningful way? Here's my challenge to you: practice reaching out to one real person every day, not just as an exercise, but as a powerful strategy to grow your business.

You wrote your book for one real person, right?

Now you need to go and find one real person per day and wow them!

Your book is not just the pages it's written on – it is a tailored solution, a response to their unique needs, wants and challenges. You've stepped into their shoes, viewed the world through their eyes, and emerged with an understanding so profound it found its way into your book. Your book, then, becomes a potent tool, a personalised gift that speaks to them, resonates with them and earns you a space in their memory.

This is the all heart, "one real person strategy" – the simplest and most effective way of expanding your influence. When you send them your book, signed and annotated with personalised notes, they feel seen, acknowledged and valued. It is an act of giving, yet not a handout. It creates an important distinction in their mind – it's a real gift, not a freebie.

This approach can transform the way you do business, becoming an essential part of your discovery calls or onboarding.

The one real person strategy works because you know what their problems are.

People generally face two types of problems: urgent, immediate crises, referred to as "bleeding neck" problems, and subtler, persistent problems, what I call "weeping wound" problems[1]. Bleeding neck problems are like imminent health or business risks, or pressing personal dilemmas, characterised by urgency and life-altering consequences. Weeping wounds consist of long-term concerns like maintaining fitness as we age, striking a work-life balance through outsourcing, or reflecting on one's life quality. These are not immediately disastrous but can escalate if left unaddressed.

A third category, and one we often forget to address, are those "invisible" problems, the deep-seated worries and fears that often invade your thoughts during sleepless nights. I call these the "4 a.m. Dave Brain"[2] problems, that show up on repeat night after night. These issues include self-doubts, fear of failure, existential queries and other puzzling concerns that wake you up at four in the morning.

Because you have deeply understood the one real person's problem this is the easiest and most effective way of growing your business. You've researched their needs so they feel seen and understood. Heck, you wrote the book for them!

> **Stop selling the book. Share the solution to their bleeding neck, weeping wound or Dave Brain problem.**

Problems (and solutions) of the all heart, one real person strategy

Problems you might encounter:

1. It might be difficult to find more people like your "one person". And even if you do, it might be difficult to find their mailing address.

2. You might not have the budget to send one book per day, especially if you're traditionally published.

3. You might feel like a stalker. Or that you're black-mailing people.

> **Share your book with your one real person, the wonderful human being you wrote your book for.**

Solutions:

1. Ask your *original* one person. They have hang-out places in real life and online. They follow and subscribe to influencers, newsletters and YouTube channels. They know other people, like them, who should get a copy of your book. They will be proud and excited to help you – just ask them. They might even want some copies to give away themselves; now you're tapping into their network (see strategy two).

2. Even if your publishing deal means the cost of printed books is prohibitive, you might be able to give away PDF copies. It doesn't have the same impact as a lovely gift turning up in the post, but it's a good second best.

3. Get over yourself. If you sent me a printed copy of your book, as long as it is relevant, I'd be over the moon. If the person thinks you're doing something nefarious,[3] do you really want to do business with them anyway?

It's scary out there

Many authors do nothing with their books because of fear. They convince themselves that nothing is OK. But what are we all so scared about? These are my biggest fears, the fears of my clients, and some made up ones to make sure you're paying attention:

1. Spending money on gaining attention (adverts, offers, social media) and not making it back.
2. Looking desperate to our peers, competitors and worse of all, our clients.
3. Being judged by people we respect because of our noisy marketing.
4. Clowns, spiders and priests.
5. Doing the wrong thing.
6. Doing the right thing wrong.

This is why the all heart, one real person tactic is so great.

1. Only one real person at a time will see your person-alised message and the book.
2. Only one person to judge you; you're not shouting into the noise.
3. If it doesn't work you don't have an audience spectating.
4. People really aren't watching you that much – they're too busy wondering if their bum looks big or why that priest is dressed as a clown.

The "all heart" tactic

If you use discovery calls and meetings as part of the sales process for your business, then before a call you can send them a book. It will be an impressive introduction to who you are and what you can offer. Following the call or meeting, the book reinforces the connection established during the conversation. In this manner, one real person at a time, you sow the seeds of growth and form a network of meaningful relationships.

7. Hyper-personalised, one real person

This is my favourite strategy. I love thinking about people, surprising them, making them happy. Your book can do all three.

It takes a bit more time and energy from your point of view and doesn't make the big splashes like getting a bestseller, billions of books sold or seven million reviews. However, I think this is probably the most sensible and sensitive way for all of my clients to grow their business with their book.

Find one person who should read your book, send them the book with a handwritten note and some stickies on appropriate pages. "I thought you'd love the 'one real person' strategy in the final chapter. I've added a sticky so you can read it straight away". Be genuine, real, enthusiastic.

> You can up the ante with this technique by sending two copies. One for your one real person, and another for them to gift to someone they think should read it. Sometimes, the person who needs to read your book may not be the person you think it is. Give a "twofer[4]"!

Just like gourmet cooking, memorable haircuts, or those unforgettable first dates, the in-person, highly person-alised approach works best. **It's like sending a hand-crafted love letter, one book at a time.**

> If you've learnt anything useful from me or my books, please take a moment to let me know as a review or testimonial. (This is a request, and a suggestion for you to add similar words to your book or book page.)

If you're feeling ambitious, put the book in a shiny envelope or a branded box. In the late '90s this was my go-to move at the end of speaking gigs. I would have a table at the back of the room with just ten (scarcity) bright red, shiny envelopes (intrigue). Inside was my book and some special offers. People would queue to get a hold of a copy (of course there were more under the desk), pay their money and check what was inside the envelope. Special package magic! Piers Fallowfield-Cooper, executive coach and author of *Are You Still The Future?* says: "*Sending a signed book with a personalised note to the right person is fifty times better than a boring book from Amazon. I always frame the concept of my book with a quote from a fan to encourage the recipient to read it.*"

The keys to this tactic:

1. Find the right people. Start with your inner circle, then have a process for asking for addresses for sending before or after discovery calls. If you don't do calls, find people who should get a copy of your book and make them an offer.

2. Highlight specific paragraphs or explanations that are useful to them, or a different way that they can be thinking about their problem. Be hyper-personal.

3. Send the books. Use a mailing service or a VA when you've got the tactic going. For your first fifty, find time to do this yourself. The first fifty people you think of will probably be in your inner circle, so the extra personalised touch will be appreciated.

4. And follow up with them. Call them. Did you read the book? What did you think about the story in chapter 4? Who else should read a copy?

5. Do one send out per day for the first three months. Get at least sixty copies out there in the hands of people who will do business with you or refer you.

> You may be worried that your hyper-personalised book won't get to the right person. This is especially tricky if you're trying to get your book to CEOs or leaders in larger organisations, where their incoming post may get reviewed. The way to ensure your book gets to the right person is to use the special package magic trick, that way it won't look like normal post, it will appear personal, it will get through.

Jean-Charles Savornin[5] uses his books as a person to person exchange. He knows his books are valuable and informative, when he meets with a potential client he leaves them with a book. It takes the business card to the next level. I advise all my clients to follow this strategy.

> Remember, it all hinges on the fabulous follow up. Invite questions, get them on a call, solicit a review or endorsement, and ask who else they know who should read your book.

Want to go even further in the hyper-personalisation? If you have self-published (or cohort published) then you can take this to the next level. Add ten pages to your book files, then for every client re-write those pages as a hyper-hyper-personalised (is that hyper to the power of two?) proposal. Talk about their particular issues, and how your methodology solves them. Upload your files to IngramSpark and print out copies for the deciding team to read. That's a proposal that will never get thrown away, and much better than a brochure.

It's impossible to be afraid of sending a book to someone you like. This is the easiest strategy for breaking the "do nothing" barrier of fear.

ENDNOTES

1. Perry Marshall in Sell or Die first coined the phrase "bleeding neck"; I think I made up "weeping wound" and it appeared first in my book *Stop writing books nobody reads*.

2. Sorry to all the Daves out there, but don't blame me, blame the BBC. "Dave" is a British television channel, which is available in the UK and Ireland.

3. I'm happy to say I've finally used the word nefarious in a book. Thank you for your indulgence.

4. Two for the price of one (almost).

5. *Arrêtez de suivre vos projets...Pilotez-les*, Jean-Charles Savornin, self-published.

8. STOP (ONLY) SELLING BOOKS – AND THE EIGHTH TACTIC TO AVOID

You've read everything (because this is a short valuable book which means you can get through it in a couple of hours), so what should you do now? If you do nothing you've had a quick read and an insight into my chaotic mind.

Before you leave I want you to consider that there are eight different things you can do to move your book. I've shown you the four strategies with their seven tactics. The eighth is: Do Nothing! Yes, you can do nothing. You don't have to market your book, I'm not going to tell anyone. You don't have to make a difference with your ideas, it's not the law. You are the boss of you and your book.

I think it would be a shame if you didn't get a return on your investment, if you didn't capitalise on your asset. But, you need to work the asset to get a return on your investment. You wouldn't buy a house and leave it to rot or not use it. It's the same with your book asset.

One by one
    1. Low cost book bundle
    2. Book plus upsell

One to many
    3. Partnerships
    4. Sponsors

Strategically free
    5. Free ebook
    6. Free + shipping

Hyper-personalised
    7. One real person

8. Do nothing!

If you do decide to do something then remember:

- You don't need to only do one of the strategies, you can do more or all.
- Any of these tactics can be running at the same time.
- But don't do all of them at once – that would be bonkers.
- You don't need to do everything yourself; you're a thought leader not a website designer (unless you're a website designer).

- You don't need to continue with a tactic if it doesn't work for you. You're the boss of you.
- Which is why you need to measure, iterate and refine, so you can make good decisions.
- But you do need to do something because your book isn't going to sell itself.

My advice is to start with strategy four, the one real person, get that running and check your results. At the same time, pick any one of the others and give it a good shot for six months, see what the results are, and adjust on the way. Think in quarterly campaigns, rather than years. In the diagram you can see how some strategies become very expensive depending upon your publishing method. In fact. some may be prohibited, always make sure you check with your publishing partner.

	1: 👤	1: 👥	∅	♡+
Traditional	~~💲💲~~	✕ *Prohibited**	✕ *Prohibited**	✓
Hybrid	~~💲~~	?	?	✓
Self-publish or Cohort	✓	✓	✓	✓

* Might be prohibited – read your contract

How to stop selling books nobody buys

Your checklist:

- ✓ Select a tactic for the next quarter (your timing constraint)
- ✓ Select an outcome (what you are measuring)
- ✓ Make a list of the actions needed to complete the tactic (don't be scared, if it works you only need to do these once)
- ✓ Allocate resources (time, money, people)
- ✓ Measure the things that matter (you're in control of the leading numbers, and a spectator for the lagging)
- ✓ Execute to the best of your ability with enthusiasm and vigour (if you don't believe in your book why should they?)

> **Get your own copy of the Book Marketing Canvas™ from www.shortvaluablebooks.com**

These strategies are just tools you can pick up and use. They're designed to run concurrently, bolstering one another. You can turn the heat up on your book marketing or turn it down. Add tactics or remove them. Think of them as sprints, not marathons. But caution is key – attempting all of them at once would be an exercise in madness, not efficiency. Chain them for best results.

Chaining campaigns reduces the downward tendency, so you never end up back in the low incoming leads with a low (or no!) pay off section of the graph. Each campaign builds on the success of the last, keeping the soup simmering.

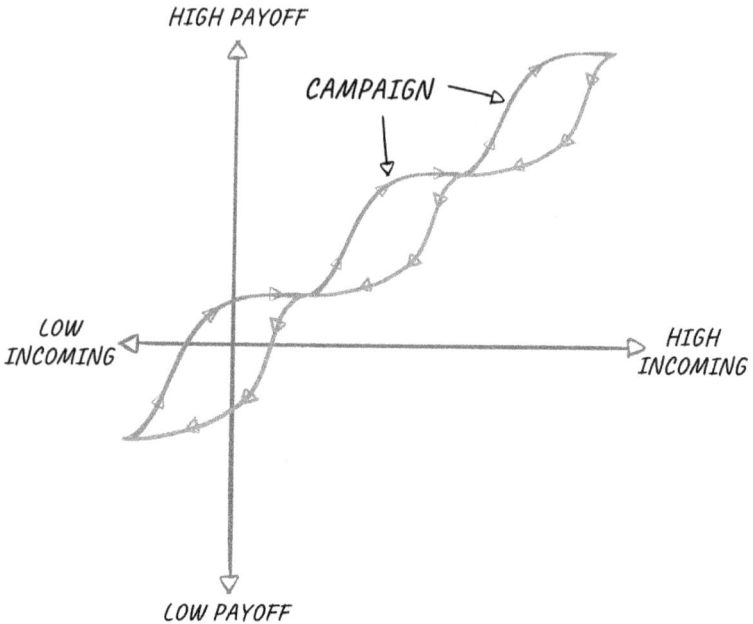

As a thought leader, your strength lies in your vision, not in micromanaging every aspect of implementation. It's perfectly acceptable to delegate tasks that fall outside your expertise or comfort zone. Select tactics that you can implement, test, and then pass on to someone (or something) else to manage. You can outsource to a VA, SAAS or an AI[1]. It's not only okay but smart!

Books, as marvellous as they may be, cannot sell themselves. Your engagement is critical in getting your book into the hands of the people who need to read it. You're the bridge between your book and those who will benefit from its wisdom.

The journey to success isn't a mad dash. It's more like a pot of soup, simmering gently to perfection. It's a game of patience and persistence, gently adjusting the flame, never letting it die out. Stay the course, keep faith in your journey, and remember, your greatest allies are your enduring spirit and adaptability (and coffee, coffee really helps).

ENDNOTES

1. That might be the shortest sentence with the most acronyms I've ever written. Virtual Assistant, Software as a Service and Artificial Intelligence.

WHO IS DEBBIE JENKINS?

As a kid, I devoured second hand, thumbed copies of the Bible, Isaac Asimov, the revised 13th edition of Encyclopedia Britannica (except PAS-PLA, missing in action) and the Reader's Digests. I knew I'd end up doing something with books, despite a careers advisor warning me against it.

The first publishing business I started in 2004, specialised in publishing unique non-fiction titles by genuine experts and thought leaders with niche books that, although mainstream publishers tend to overlook, were packed with information hungry readers wanted. At the heart of everything we did was fair play and efficiency. We worked hard to create a virtuous circle and put profit back into our authors' pockets while building a viable business ourselves. I exited that company in 2011, and they've gone on to do even greater things.

I love working with smart consultants, coaches and mentors who are brilliant at serving their clients, and also need to take care of their own practice. I've been running my own consultancy businesses for the last 25+ years. My first business was a digital marketing agency in the '90s helping consultants, coaches, trainers, speakers and expert advisors to grow their business while reducing marketing waste. Over the next 3 years I grew that company to 12 employees, an office in the city, a chillax room for the team... I thought I knew what I was doing. But I missed capitalising on a vital step – I didn't create enough assets that would work for me so that I didn't have to keep on selling my own and my team's time.

I know that it's easy to get caught up delivering to clients, keeping on top of trends and technology, marketing and proposal writing, racing from job to job. It's hard to squeeze in time for your own personal professional development, let alone find space to think about creating assets. And there's the dilemma, because without these assets you'll always be bouncing from job to job, selling your time not your value, and leaving your best ideas on your busy desk.

Over the last 25 years I have helped COOs from Microsoft, VPs from McDonald's and Executives from Mars (the company, not the planet) create, build and launch assets that have helped them win clients, build their personal practices and become published authors*.

Through my publishing company I published over 80 business books.

After I sold it I went on to help more than 30 smart business owners write their legacy book, and coached hundreds of consultants to market themselves, their business, and their IP. I have ghostwritten bestselling business books for venture capitalists, CFOs, MBEs, professors, mentors and coaches. I have designed and marketed apps, produced websites and written/co- written more than 20 books (my first in 2003). In the last few years, I have had coaching clients get published with Bloomsbury, Pearson, Business Expert Press, BIS, and Taylor & Francis. Other coaching clients chose themselves, decided the best route would be to use a hybrid publisher, or they've self-published. Each route to publishing is valid and has its own pros and cons. Now, I'm helping experts get their book written and published through my own publishing company, Intellectual Perspective Press.

I know how to help you get the clever ideas out of your head (or off your computer) and turned into valuable things (assets) for your business. Assets like business books, whitepapers, converting websites, marketing materials, podcasts … I also know how to help you use these assets to accelerate your time to impact, achieve visibility and influence, and improve your bottom line – that is The Asset Path.

I have a 1st Class Degree in Electronics Engineering which means I am trained to look for sustainable and innovative solutions to problems, I understand technology and software development, and I can create models and frameworks that people can use (and I know what a MOSFET is). I moved to Southern Spain in 2005. I live at the Disaster Farm (that's not a typo) with a host of animals, where I invite special clients to visit and work on their assets in person. I only work ten months of the year because the Disaster Farm needs my attention too – and if I don't take a break who's going to hand feed the horses juicy carrots and lounge around reading all those books I've bought?

I am determined to help all my clients make the most of their IP, ideas and talent. I can help you turn your clever ideas into valuable things. And we'll have fun doing it.

* I work with people from companies that don't start with an M too!

THERE'S ALWAYS A PS: TECHNICAL KNOW-HOW AND THE ROBOTS

I am renowned (in my own mind) for writing things in parentheses (like this) and always having a PS at the end of my newsletter. So I thought I'd share a really useful PS with you: the technical know-how section.

> **This section is available in all its clicky goodness (and will be updated) on www.shortvaluablebooks.com**

I'll share the most useful and current (these things change rapidly) tech stacks that could work for you, and tell you what I'm using for my own business and for my clients.

My advice: keep it as simple as you can. I am a mistress of overcomplification, and rarely take my own tech advice because I love playing (the engineer in me), but if you don't have a tech department just keep it simple.

Get your book website working:
Thrive Themes and Thrive Cart (they are not the same company): for all my website goodness. Thrive Themes

sits on top of a Wordpress site and gives it extra powers. Thrive Cart lets me take money for purchases of ebooks, books, courses, memberships.

Stripe Products: perhaps the simplest way of taking credit card payments. You set up a product and embed or link to the payment form from your website or email.

Clickfunnels and Carrd: if you want a one page site or a dedicated sales page, Clickfunnels and Carrd sit at the opposite ends of the scales in functionality and price. I've used both, they each have their advantages.

Sending emails:
Activecampaign, Mailchimp, Mailerlite: these are my preferred mailing solutions. They all let you capture email addresses legally, set up message flows, and segment the contacts.

Creating quizzes, diagnostics and tests:
Scoreapp, Thrive Quiz Builder, SQB: from one extreme of cost to the other, they have plenty of similarities. I use all three for different reasons and clients.

The Bots:
ChatGPT, Copy.ai, Bard: These are the word bots I use, I can guarantee that this list will change frequently for me. Have a look on www.shortvaluablebooks.com for the most fun and useful AI interns.

Canva, Dall-E, Miro: my image interns.

Productivity and managing the strategies:

Notion, Trello, Streak: I use all three for different parts of the process. Streak is a simple, free CRM in your gmail. Trello and Notion allow you to manage the tasks involved in any of the strategies in this book.

Creating books:

KDP.amazon.com, BookVault, IngramSpark: of course everyone knows you can sell your books with Amazon, but there are other routes to the market. You may also wish to buy bulk copies, BookVault can help with that.

Get access to all the bonuses and checklists mentioned by clicking on this link or scanning the QR code. You'll get your own copy of the Book Marketing Checklist and an up to date list of useful technology to help you.

ACKNOWLEDGEMENTS

Books don't write themselves, and they're rarely solo endeavours. This book started life as coaching calls with my wonderful clients, which turned into a short presentation, that morphed into a sprint for authors.

Thanks to all my authors for stirring the pot and helping me avoid the clowns.

Thanks most of all to the wonderful Asset Path team of: Jayr Cuario on book design and project management; Lisa de Caux for her gentle art of editing; and Amit Dey for interior design.

OTHER BOOKS BY
DEBBIE JENKINS

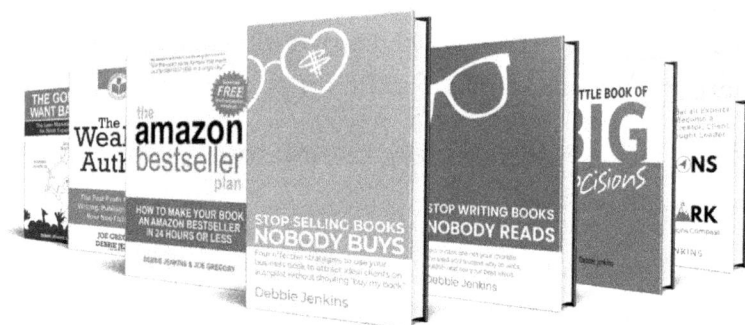

Find out about all of my books at www.DebbieJenkins.com

STILL NOT SURE WHAT TO DO?

Already an author?

If you weren't able to see how your current book was could to bring you business, grow your revenue or save you time and money, maybe you need to go back to book writing class. Not the fairy-tale type of writing, but the sensible, business-growing book writing. I have a community of leaders who join me for regular strategy calls: OnlyAuthors.club

Want to write a book?

Write your next book with my team as part of a Publishing Cohort. We regularly start a new cohort of smart leaders and consultants, who are ready and prepared to get their valuable ideas tested, written and published. There's a waitlist, join us at: expertauthor.academy

Want to keep in touch?

I run the "Ideas into Assets: Effective advice on writing and publishing your business growing book" with new topics weekly on Wednesdays throughout the year. You can get your access link at www.shortvaluablebooks.com

What do we want?
A book that is read and referred, searched for and shared, desired and devoured.
When do we want it?
Now!
What are we prepared to do to get it?

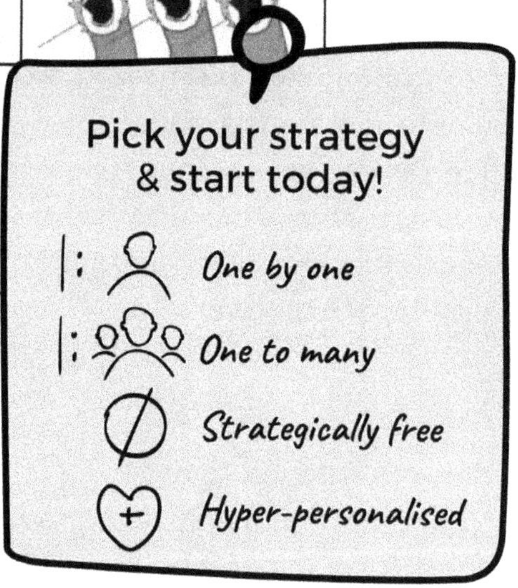
Pick your strategy & start today!
One by one
One to many
Strategically free
Hyper-personalised